THE
FINANCIAL
GUIDE FOR
THE SINGLE
PARENT

Larry Burkett

REVISED AND EXPANDED

MOODY PRESS
CHICAGO

ACKNOWLEDGMENT

I want to thank Brenda Armstrong, Christian Financial Concepts' director of single parents ministries, for her unique assistance in the updating and revision of this book. Her years as a single parent and her experience in working with single parents were invaluable in the preparation of this book.

✍

Edited by Adeline Griffith

ISBN: 0-8024-2738-3

5 7 9 10 8 6

Printed in the United States of America

CONTENTS

INTRODUCTION

I n 1973 my family and I moved from Florida to Atlanta, Georgia. I had just left a business to join the staff of a national ministry as a financial counselor. It was during this time I began writing what later became a study on the biblical principles of handling finances.

A Christian orthodontist, Bob Lahr, invited me to share an office in his medical building. In exchange I agreed to counsel with some of his nonpaying clients. Our agreement was simple. He would accept whatever payment they were able to make, provided they would agree to meet with me monthly and stick to a budget.

I had done some financial counseling during my first three years as a Christian, although much of the time had been spent studying the Word, particularly the principles of handling money. By default I had become the resident counselor in our church on the subject of finances for two basic reasons. One, I had a business background in finances. Second, nobody else was willing to tackle the problems. I relied heavily upon the book of Proverbs for much of the counsel I gave.

I learned the meaning behind an old cliché that says, "In the land of the blind, a one-eyed man is king." I didn't know a lot about what God's Word said about finances, but I knew a lot more than most of the other Christians around me.

After counseling with mostly middle-income families, I had concluded that the vast majority of financial problems were the result of mismanaging the funds that were available. In most instances, if I could just get them to handle their funds logically, they could easily get out of debt and even develop a surplus of money. As long as my counseling was limited to middle-income families or above, that premise held true.

In Atlanta I came face-to-face with a new set of conditions because many of the doctor's nonpaying patients were single parents, primarily divorcees who sought orthodontic treatment for their children. As I began to counsel with these individuals, I found some situations for which there seemed to be no solutions. In general, they were living on incomes that often were much less than that of other families I had counseled. These single parents had to pay the same household expenses but had the added expense of child care that most of the other families didn't have.

Small things, like minor car repairs, became major crises in their finances. Large items, such as orthodontic care, became insurmountable barriers that plunged them into debt and despair. The financial problems were compounded by feelings of hopelessness because of the situations they faced. Most had no choice but to place their children in day care in order to work. And, on top of the other problems, most of them had to deal with the guilt of failed marriages.

Over the next few years I learned a lot about the financial problems that single parents face and what others can do to help. There are specific responsibilities for the single parent prior to asking others for help; but, without outside help, the long-term prospects can get pretty grim.

In the original version of this book titled *The Complete Financial Guide to Single Parents,* I addressed the most common concerns of the single parents who were seeking counseling, who were primarily widows and divorcees, and the book offered a variety of solutions. However, it became apparent that the book needed updating when we began to see a broader set of single parent problems surfacing. The diversity of problems increased because single parent families had changed.

According to the U.S. Census in 1994, 38 percent of custodial single parents were divorced, an unprecedented 38 percent were never-married single parents, 20 percent were separated from a spouse, and 5 percent were widowed. Another factor was the dramatic increase in custodial fathers, which represented 16 percent of all single parent households.

In the following stories, we'll discuss some of the more common problems single parents face today. Topics include issues like divorce, unwed parenthood, custodial fathering, noncustodial parenting, widowhood, alimony, child support, housing, insurance, child care, and cars. The stories provide valuable lessons about the consequences of some single parenting decisions and offer insight into how the single parents overcame their desperate situations. In each case, we'll examine how the church helped—or could have helped.

The majority of references are to mothers because women still greatly outnumber men in raising children alone. They earn less than men, and they struggle more financially. In fact, single-mother families have the highest rate of poverty across all demographic groups. Seventy-three percent of children from single mother families are impoverished, compared with 20 percent of two-parent families. The average income for a single mother is less than $15,000 per year.

With more out-of-wedlock births, no-fault divorces, and uncollected or nonestablished child support, many more single mothers are raising their children without any father involvement. Forty percent of the children living in single mother homes have not seen their fathers in the last year. In fact, more than half of all the children who do not live with their fathers have never even been in their father's homes. With more "deadbeat dads" escaping responsibility, these abandoned women and children truly are the biblical widows and orphans of today, and they desperately need the church's help.

On the other hand, statistics show that only about 10 percent of all single fathers are deadbeat dads. Twenty percent of single dads live below the poverty level in income, and another 20 percent hover just above the poverty line. We don't hear much about their concerns because most single fathers will not seek help. Men are not supposed to be needy; they are supposed to be the providers for their families. The church needs to understand that although their needs are different from those of single mothers, they are just as vital to the well-being of their children.

There are many godly, committed, and caring men who want to be actively involved in the lives of their children, whether they're raising them alone or not. Of the other 60 percent who could provide for their children, many of them don't because they have been kept away from their children by their former spouse. Ninety percent of fathers with joint custody pay child support, 79 percent of fathers who frequently see their children pay support, and only 45 percent of the fathers without visitation pay support.

The single parents' names and identifying details have been changed to protect the families of those who contributed their stories; but, their perspectives, fears, and decisions remain authentic. Most single parents will be able to identify with the struggles and decisions faced by the ones whose stories we tell.

This book also was updated to accompany *The Financial Guide for the Single Parent* workbook, which explores the specific financial concerns of single parents in greater detail and walks them step-by-step through the budgeting process. It includes numerous ideas, testimonies, budgeting samples, and solutions for stretching available dollars.

Since the majority of widows are not parenting children under 18, many of them did not know about the information that was included for them in the original book. Although the needs of widows are still addressed in this book, to make the information more available, we also created a free publication called "What Every Widow Needs to Know." Not only is it helpful to widows but also to those working with widows or married women who want to be prepared for the difficult financial decisions that arise after the loss of a spouse. It is available by calling Christian Financial Concepts at 1-800-722-1976 or by downloading from CFC's Internet site (http://www.cfcministry.org).

The ongoing needs of single parents have always been a concern for me, but the daily reality hit home when my own daughter became a single parent through no fault of her own. It was tough for her, even though she had the support of her family. Many abandoned mothers do not have family support or families nearby. I've always been dismayed that so few churches do anything on a consistent basis to help meet the single parents' needs.

Our contact with churches has confirmed that most churches want to help but they don't know where to begin. As a ministry, we have addressed those concerns through our single parent department. A how-to manual was designed to train churches and communities in a development seminar how to meet the ongoing practical needs of single parents.

I hope the ministries and resources we develop not only will help single parents but also will encourage others to begin this vital type of ministry and help mobilize the resources necessary to meet the needs that can be met only through the generosity of those with a surplus.

THE TRAUMA OF DIVORCE

Marriage has become disposable for many people, like everything else in our society today. Even though vows still say "for better or worse, in sickness and in health, for richer or poorer, until death do we part," lifetime biblical commitments are rare. In fact, some people plan for the end of their marriage even before it begins.

There are many reasons for divorce: few are biblical; most are not. Whatever the cause, when divorce is spoken of as an option in a relationship, it is often inevitable. Divorce always causes destruction and pain, even for those who desire a divorce, because it tears a family apart. In the following story, Carol was oblivious to the consequences that her decisions would cause until she came face-to-face with the realities of single parenting.

NOWHERE TO TURN

Carol was married when she was just 19 years old. She and her husband Bob met in college and were married in June of Bob's junior year. In spite of the many objections by both parents, they were determined that the marriage was "God's will."

Five years later Carol found herself divorced, with little work experience, and faced with trying to support her three-year-old son. A bitter divorce left Carol and Bob at odds about everything from child support to who got the pickup truck. In reality Carol was emotionally better off than the majority of divorcees who feel like they've lost someone they really cared about. In Carol's case she had decided she would be better off without Bob. They had been fighting about almost everything, especially finances, for several years. We pick up Carol's story right after the divorce was finalized.

With Timmy's child support and what I can earn, we'll be able to rent our own place, Carol told herself. *At least I won't have to listen to Bob complain about not finishing school because, as he always says, "You went and got yourself pregnant." I wonder if he remembers that it takes two to make a baby.* "Besides," she said aloud, "Timmy's the only good thing to come out of this dumb marriage."

As Carol began her search for work she became acutely aware that salaries above $5 an hour were very limited and the job market was extremely competitive. After three weeks of searching she got a job as a waitress in a local restaurant. Her base salary was $2.50 an hour; tips brought her income up to about double that amount. As would be expected, she had a difficult time making ends meet. The first month Bob's child support payment was late, she was unable to pay her rent on time. When the 15th came and the check still had not arrived, she called Bob's apartment. It was nearly 10 P.M. and she was surprised to hear a woman answer the phone.

"Is Bob in?" Carol asked timidly.

"Who wants to know?" the brassy female voice asked.

"This is Bob's wife . . . ex-wife," Carol replied. Inside she had a cold feeling, as if something had died. Without realizing it, she had somehow thought that Bob still would be faithful to her, as she was to him.

"He's here, but he's in the shower right now. You want me to ask him somethin' for ya?"

"Just tell him I called about the check for Timmy, please," Carol said, anxious to get off the line as quickly as possible.

"I'll tell him, but don't hold your breath, Honey. He's still mad about havin' to pay for his truck. He said you'll get the money when he's good and ready."

Carol's hand was shaking as she put down the phone. She felt like she was going to throw up. She and Bob had argued bitterly, and she was even glad to be away from him, but she still felt the ties of marriage and secretly hoped they would get back together. Only, she wanted to make it on her own first, to prove to Bob that she wasn't the dummy he thought she was. Now she had the terrifying feeling that she was all alone—with her small son.

Things got more difficult for Carol over the next several months. She lived in constant fear of Timmy getting sick. With even the slightest temperature, the day school wouldn't let him stay and she would have to miss work. Twice in the last month she'd had to leave work early to get Timmy, and the manager had told her, "One more time, Carol, and you're fired. I need workers I can depend on."

"But I need this job, Mr. Hall," she had pleaded. "Timmy's not sick very often, and I know he's better now." Even as she said it, she knew that she had to keep Timmy on aspirin or his fever would return. She needed to take him to a good pediatrician, but there was never any money—or time.

Carol thought about taking Bob back to court to make him pay her more and pay on time. But the last time she threatened him he had countered, "Go ahead, Carol, and I'll take Timmy away from you. I know you're behind on your bills and you can't provide for him properly." This terrified Carol so greatly she was afraid to even call Bob again. She really was having financial problems, and she knew she couldn't give Timmy proper medical care.

One Sunday evening, Carol noticed that Timmy wasn't acting normal. Suddenly he passed out and began to convulse. She grabbed him in her arms and raced out to her car. The nearest hospital was a private treatment center only a few blocks away. Carol dashed into the emergency room with Timmy still unconscious. The emergency room doctor took Timmy and began to work on him. Within a few minutes he was back to talk to Carol.

"Mrs. West?" he asked as he entered the waiting room.

"Yes, Doctor," Carol replied. "Is Timmy okay?" she cried out.

"Yes, he is. He just went into convulsions because of his fever," the doctor replied. "He has a very bad inner ear infection. How long has he been sick?"

"I don't really know, Doctor," she replied as she sat down in a waiting room chair. "It seems like a long time now, maybe four or five months."

"Well I'm concerned that he could lose the hearing in his left ear. I'd like to keep him in the hospital a couple of days and treat that ear with antibiotics. Do you have health insurance?"

Inside, Carol panicked. She assumed if she told them the truth, that she didn't have insurance, they wouldn't let Timmy stay, since it was a private hospital. So she lied. "Yes, I do," she said. "We're covered under my husband's plan at work."

"Good," the doctor replied. "Just give your account number to the receptionist and we'll check Timmy into the pediatric ward."

Carol took the old insurance card out of her purse and gave the account code to the receptionist.

"Mrs. West, we'll need to verify the insurance with your husband's company," the receptionist said as she took down the information.

Carol felt like her heart skipped a beat.

Then the receptionist added, "Oh dear, since it's Sunday there won't be anyone at the claims office. I'll leave word for the day shift receptionist to check. But I'm sure it will be all right. Your husband is still employed at the same company, isn't he?"

"Yes, he is," Carol answered, without adding, "but he's not my husband anymore." Carol felt a flush of anger inside. *Bob could have kept us on his policy,* she thought, *but he refused. The judge said he had to be responsible for Timmy's bills, but I know he'll try to make me out to be a bad mother, just for spite.*

With Timmy safely checked into the pediatric ward, Carol went home in total mental exhaustion. The next morning she called the hospital to check on Timmy before she went to work. She was afraid to go by and see him for fear they would find out about the phony insurance and dismiss him. She asked for the pediatric nurse and asked how Timmy West was doing.

"He's doing fine, Mrs. West," the nurse replied. "He's asleep right now and should sleep for several more hours. Poor little guy, he was just worn out from fighting the infection."

"Thank you," Carol said with a rush of relief inside. "Please tell him I'll be by right after work. And tell him I love him very much."

"I'll do that, Mrs. West," the nurse replied. "And don't you worry about a thing, he'll be fine now."

Carol spent a fitful day at work. She was alternately caught between a feeling of relief, knowing that Timmy was getting the treatment he needed, and the feeling of dread, knowing that by now the hospital must have verified that she didn't have any insurance.

That morning time seemed to drag by as Carol worried about her son. But the afternoon seemed to fly by, and she dreaded the confrontation she knew was coming when she went to visit Timmy that evening. Her mind conjured up images of the hospital having her arrested and the court taking Timmy away from her. She was a nervous wreck by quitting time. When she arrived at the hospital and asked where Timmy's room was, the lady in pink at the desk asked, "What did you say his name is, dear?"

"It's Timmy West," Carol repeated.

The volunteer scrolled through the names on her computer screen until she came to Timmy West. Then she said, "Mrs. West, you'll have to see Mr. Harms, the administrator. Apparently there is some kind of error in your admission form."

Carol dreaded the meeting that she knew was coming. She walked slowly down the hall to the administrator's office. She knocked on the door and heard, "Come in."

Carol introduced herself, "I'm Carol West, Timmy's mother."

"Ah yes, Mrs. West," he said, looking at the account notice on his desk. "It seems we have some kind of mix-up in your insurance. According to the insurance company, your son Timmy was dropped from the policy nearly nine months ago, when you and your husband were divorced."

"That's true," Carol admitted as the tears formed up in her eyes. "I lied because I was afraid they wouldn't admit Timmy for treatment last night."

"But Mrs. West, this is a private hospital and we're not equipped for welfare patients. The county hospital is funded for patients who are unable to afford medical care."

"We're not on welfare!" Carol snapped defensively. "I apologize for deceiving you, but I didn't know what else to do at the time."

"Well I'm afraid your son won't be able to stay unless someone guarantees payment on the bill," the administrator said with finality. "I'm sorry but that is the hospital's policy."

"Could I arrange credit with the hospital?" Carol pled. "I don't want Timmy moved now."

"No, I'm sorry. Hospital policy requires that all credit must be approved in advance. However, we do accept all major credit cards for payment. Do you have one?"

Carol knew that she still had three credit cards from when she was married. *But how will I ever pay them off?* she thought as her mind raced through the options available. She then made a decision that was to drastically affect the rest of her finances. "Yes, I do. I have Visa and MasterCard." The total bill for Timmy's care came to just under $4,000, which took both of her credit cards to the maximum limit.

The next month was filled with anxiety as Carol waited for the bills to arrive. In the meantime the brakes on her car began to make an awful noise. She continued to drive until finally the screech was continuous and the brakes smelled like burning rubber. She dropped the car off at the small garage near her work to have them checked.

When she returned to pick up her car that evening the mechanic said, "The bill on your car is $600, Mrs. West. You drove it too long on worn-out brakes and scored the rotors. We had to put on new ones."

"Six hundred dollars!" Carol shouted. "I don't have $600! How could it be that much?"

"That's what it took," the mechanic said rudely. "This ain't no charity work here, you know. We have a loan company that will lend the money for repairs if you own your car. You do own this car, don't you?"

"Yes," Carol said as she began to cry.

Inside she felt as if she had dropped into a pit of despair. *Another loan,* she thought. *I can't pay the loans I already have. I can't even pay the rent this month. It doesn't seem to ever stop.*

By the end of the next month Carol was shifting money from one creditor to another just to keep them off her back. Even without the credit card payments and the small loan company debt, she needed nearly $200 a month more than she made. One evening she returned from a long day on her feet to find a note from her landlord saying that if she didn't pay her rent she would be evicted immediately. Fearful of being put out on the street, she took the reserve she had been saving for Timmy's day school and gave it to the apartment complex manager. It didn't cover the entire amount due, but Carol promised to have the remainder by the next paycheck.

The next day, as she dropped Timmy off at school, she was met by the school administrator. "Carol, you're over a month behind on Timmy's bill now," she said. "If you don't get caught up by the end of this month, we won't be able to keep him any longer."

"I'll do my best, Mrs. Roberts," Carol said, fighting back the tears and despair. *Oh God,* she thought to herself, *I wish I were dead. I never thought things would get this bad.*

That day at work one of Carol's regular customers came into the diner for his usual lunch. He was an older man who owned a successful package delivery business. He picked out his favorite booth. "What are you so down in the dumps about, Carol? You've been draggin' around for the last few days like you lost your only friend."

Carol was near tears anyway, and she began to unload all that had happened to her over the last several months since her divorce. "I just don't know what I'll do," she said through the tears. "If they put Timmy out of the day school, I won't be able to work."

"Why don't you come and live with me?" he said. "I have a large home and nobody but me lives there. With what you'd save on rent and utilities you could make it."

"Why I couldn't do that!" Carol exclaimed indignantly. "I could never just live with someone I'm not married to."

"Well, I'm not looking to get married," Carl said bluntly. "I tried it once and I don't ever intend to make that mistake again. You think it over, Carol. If you change your mind, let me know. I think it would work out okay. Besides, what other choices do you have? You want to end up on welfare or have your ex take your kid away from you?"

Carol knew that the idea of living with someone just to pay her bills went against everything she had been taught growing up in her parents' home. They were Christians, although they usually didn't attend church except Easter and other special days. They had sent her off to Sunday School regularly until she was about 13. After that she had attended sporadically. Finally, before leaving for college, she quit going to church altogether.

The more she thought about it that afternoon, the more she

realized that she had very few other options. She might call her ex-husband, but it was unlikely he would help. She thought about calling her mom, but that always ended with an argument. She had often said, "You married that bum, now you live with it." By that evening Carol had decided that she really didn't have a choice. *After all,* she told herself, *it's not that uncommon today.*

Unfortunately Carol's situation is being repeated with increasing regularity across the country. If the truth were known, many naive Christians would be shocked to find out that there are single men and women who are professing believers and even attend their churches regularly who have established an immoral lifestyle, based almost exclusively on economic necessity.

It is not my purpose to point an accusing finger at these women. Obviously, it's wrong and most of them know it. What they need is a reasonable alternative. It's not enough to just say, "They shouldn't get themselves trapped in situations where they are willing to compromise." They need a workable plan and some financial help.

A PRINCIPLE TO REMEMBER
God is your source, not people.

"Do not be anxious then, saying, 'What shall we eat?' or 'What shall we drink?' or 'With what shall we clothe ourselves?' For all these things the Gentiles eagerly seek; for your heavenly Father knows that you need all these things. But seek first His kingdom and His righteousness; and all these things shall be added to you" (Matthew 6:31-33).

A BETTER EXAMPLE
Sue couldn't understand how she ended up married to a man she didn't really know. Sure, she knew before she married him there were some problems, but most young couples had problems. She was sure her understanding and love would help to change Jim. Instead, his constant criticism and anger were becoming more hateful and she was afraid of him, especially when he was drinking.

Sue's dad was an alcoholic, so she knew what an alcoholic was like: they drank constantly, often became violent, and eventually became very ill. Her mother had told her that her dad was sick and he really couldn't help it; they just had to learn to live with it. Sue thought that if her mom cared enough about herself and her kids she would leave and try to make a better life for them, but she knew her mom wouldn't leave him. She was a Christian and would stay even if it killed her. Sue's parents didn't attend church, but they sent Sue and the other children to church on a bus every Sunday. Sue prayed earnestly that God would change her family. Sometimes in her father's rages, she secretly prayed that he would die.

Then when Sue was 16, she watched helplessly as her father died of alcoholism at age 45. Her mother died soon after that; the strain and loss were just too much for her. Sue decided then and there that she would never watch another person she loved commit suicide with alcohol.

What she didn't expect was the loneliness and pain she began to feel in her grief. Her anger at her parents just wouldn't seem to go away. She was only 18. How could they desert her like that? How could they do this to themselves? How was she going to take care of herself? It just wasn't fair! She became angry at God, her church, her family—everything and everybody. She felt like everyone had abandoned her. Her pain led her into several harmful situations. With her judgment impaired by her past and her grief, she decided she didn't want to be alone anymore. She would get married!

Sue had only known Jim a few weeks, but already she could see there was something special about him. It could have been the way he fell instantly in love with her and said all the things she wanted and needed to hear. "You're the most beautiful woman I've ever met," he told her. "I've dreamed about meeting someone like you."

Or it could have been that familiar vulnerability that caught her attention: "I need someone like you in my life." Or it could have been that he saw her pain and wanted to be there for her: "You're going to be all right. You have a lot to offer, a lot of love to give."

He was newly discharged from active service, after serving during the Vietnam war, and was just beginning to establish his life as a civilian. While in Vietnam, to help him deal with all the death and destruction he saw, he had begun using drugs and drinking. He said many service personnel did. Besides, he didn't drink or do drugs all the time, and he knew he could quit with her help. He assured Sue that what he needed was a normal family life and he would quit. Sue was so sure they could have it. Besides, Jim came from a middle-class family. As a poor, inner-city kid, she knew there was another world out there and this was her chance to experience it. Maybe now they both would have "normal" lives.

They had a couple of kids right away and, for a while, Jim kept his word; he didn't drink. He proved to be much more strict than Sue when it came to disciplining the children and told her she was just too soft. She thought he must be doing the right thing, because whenever they were in public everyone commented on what well-behaved children they had.

After a few years, a certain familiar sadness came over the kids. They only seemed happy when their dad was away. And by the time the children were adolescents, he was gone a lot.

Financial pressures had begun to mount. Sue and Jim bought their first home when the kids were small. It was a great little home in the country. They borrowed money to buy a used car to accommodate their growing family. Then Jim decided he needed a car for work so Sue wouldn't be stranded at home without transportation. So he borrowed again for a new all-terrain vehicle. Their hand-me-down furniture was beginning to fall apart under the strain of toddlers, so they borrowed again for some new furniture. Jim had a good-paying factory job, and Sue really believed him when he said they could afford all those things. She wasn't used to this lifestyle so she had to accept his judgment.

They probably would have been able to keep up the payments if it hadn't been for Jim's drinking and spending. He had expensive tastes and lots of hobbies. Every season he bought the newest and latest hunting equipment. Every Christmas or birthday he celebrated with alcohol, his defense being that he put the meat on the table, he was the provider, and he worked hard and deserved a little pleasure. Sue couldn't argue with that. After all, she was a stay-at-home mom.

The house was deteriorating and payments were past due. Sometimes the water or gas was shut off because he'd spent the money. She never bought herself anything. She spent any money he gave her on food and clothes for the kids.

It was the drinking that really began to bother her. Her fears of abandonment grew each time he drank. When he didn't come home at night her fears intensified. When she told him about her fears and asked him why he did it, he would tell her the pressures of family life and work were just too much. She just needed to understand that he needed this time to deal with things. He wasn't her father and he wouldn't leave her.

Sue saw what pressure could do to him and, in turn, what he did to the family. She certainly would do everything she could to help alleviate stress. She had to learn to stop associating Jim and her dad. She really needed to do something about her problem.

Sue was becoming very depressed. Through the years, her denial started slowly eroding. The patterns she'd developed to handle Jim weren't as effective as they once were. Things were getting worse and she didn't know how to stop them. She tried over and over to talk to him, but somehow he always turned it around to her problems or just left the house or hit something. Once, he had taken her car out drinking and someone had stolen it. The police located it, and on the trip to pick it up she thought she'd give it another try.

"Jim, I'm having some problems dealing with our marriage right now. Can we talk?" she asked cautiously, careful to judge his responses correctly.

"Sure. What's up?" he answered cheerfully.

"Well, it's not that I'm unhappy with you as a husband," she said as she searched for the right words to continue. "You can be very loving—when you want to be. It's just that, well, sometimes you scare me. I mean, what if they hurt you or killed you to get the car? And what about that woman they found driving the car? Who was she?"

"What are you getting at, Suzy Q?" He still seemed cheerful, but that could be deceiving. He always seemed to be prepared with all the answers.

She proceeded slowly and carefully to explain. "Well, you said you were with friends at a hotel playing cards, but I heard you tell the police you didn't know the people you were with. The police say the car was found in the possession of a young woman who said you *gave* her the car. You told me you didn't know who it was and that some-one must have put something in your drink and knocked you out. What am I supposed to believe?"

"You're supposed to believe your husband, not some thief who fed the police a big lie to get off the hook. Besides if I had told the police I knew the people, they would have thought I had something to do with it. Really, Suz, I don't see what the big deal is. People get their cars stolen every day. Don't you think there are thieves out there? I thought you trusted me!" His anger and hurt were pretty apparent. She knew she was treading on thin ice. One more push and he could get violent.

"I do trust you and I want to believe you." She just couldn't let it go. "But I still think your drinking is a problem. Things happen when you drink too much. Remember how you treated the kids when you got home last night? They're becoming afraid of you." She was beg-ging him to help her understand, to make some sense of it.

Now he was really hurt and defensive. "Listen, if you think my drinking is a problem, why don't you just leave? You know you'd never make it out there without me. You don't even have a job. Besides, how are you going to raise kids, taking all those depression drugs? The court would never let you have them."

He could see his remarks had hit home. Sue was shrinking back. Then suddenly his tone changed. His face softened. He added gently, almost sweetly, "I'd probably just end up in jail or dead without you. I love you, Suz, but I can't take your not trusting me, especially with my own kids! Kids need correction. You're too easy on them."

Sue was on the defensive now, "I just want to know what's going on, Jim! I know you love me and the kids. I just think something's got to change. Maybe there's something we can do. Maybe counseling. Maybe church. I don't know. I just want us to work it out. I can't han-dle it. All I want is a happy family." She began to cry. She felt weak and hopeless.

With an almost fatherly tone he answered, "If you can't handle my drinking, I'll quit. I don't drink all the time anyway. But you need to realize there's nothing wrong with drinking. It's legal, and I'm not your dad. Maybe you should go to counseling. You just need to learn how to deal with it. But personally, I really don't want a stranger knowing our business. I'd rather we work this out ourselves. I'm really sorry if I hurt you. I really love you. You're the best thing that ever happened to me."

To Sue, he really seemed to love her and he really wanted to make things better. But the incidents of hotel stays, drinking bouts, and violence just increased. When she finally got to the point that she didn't recognize the person she thought she had married, she sought counseling on her own. She began to recognize the patterns of alcoholism and break through her denial. She started making changes in the way she responded to Jim. She started establishing limits on his abusive behavior. Then, through friends in her support group, she went back to church.

Sue was overwhelmed by the love she experienced from the God she felt had abandoned her so long ago. She realized He had never left her; she had left Him. She also realized that if she chose to follow God she would probably lose Jim. She had placed Jim and reacting to him above everything, including God. She knew she had to choose God. She knew that it was the only way to have what she really needed and wanted: real love and a happy family life. After more counseling and prayer, she began to realize that she never really had Jim's love. Alcohol was always his first love.

When Jim saw the changes he was angry and, probably for the first time, he was scared that he would lose Sue. He threatened. He yelled. He promised. He even went to counseling for a few weeks and to AA. He finally told Sue that if she didn't go back to the way she was he was leaving her and filing for divorce.

Sue was terrified. All she ever wanted was a happy family. She kept trying to tell him that, but he didn't seem to get it. She told him she couldn't go back to the way she was; she would die. In fact she had already died inside a long time ago. She begged him to understand and keep working on their marriage, but he left. He filed for bankruptcy, filed for divorce, and moved in with a woman he'd met at a bar.

Sue felt helpless to stop the course that she'd begun. It hurt tremendously to see that she was so easily replaced. She only felt hope when she spent time in prayer or in her group. She lost the house, the furniture, and the car. Only a few pieces of leftover hand-me-downs were left. She was back where she started ten years before: alone and poor, with no credit and no education, and now with kids to raise.

* * * * * * * * * * * *

Unfortunately, Sue's story is very common today. Almost every family in America is affected by the effects of alcohol or drug abuse. These abandoned women, and sometimes men, need a lot of emotional healing, people who care, and financial support. In Sue's case, what she thought was the end of her life was just the beginning.

She found people who really cared about her in her church. She was given a good foundation for living, based on God's Word. She was learning how to forgive her ex-husband and to trust God to be the father and provider in her home. Although she faced some very lean times, God supplied her needs. Even though her church, family, and friends didn't really understand her ongoing needs, they helped as much as they could.

Over the years, Sue was given four cars by friends or church members, one after another as they each wore out. A church member worked on her cars and only charged her for parts. Sue's brothers helped her move and did some repair work on her cars. Someone else from church anonymously adopted her and bought her new clothes and gave her expensive department store cosmetics.

Sue didn't take her problems to the church very often. She didn't want to be dependent on the church. Instead, she confided in a few friends who would pray with her. Even though they could not meet her needs, they encouraged her to believe that God would. Many times God provided without anyone knowing the specific need.

Sue's children were always complaining that they never had anything to eat. She discounted it, mostly because all kids say that when they look in the refrigerator. But one day she went to the refrigerator and discovered she really didn't have anything to fix for dinner. She also didn't have any money.

She and her children prayed together about God's promise of provision. She could honestly say that her family was never hungry again. And many times she had so much she had to share it with others.

One member occasionally dropped off groceries on her doorstep.

Sue knew who it was and appreciated the fact that they always brought healthy food. However, her son really wanted to have "teen" food. He specifically wanted hamburgers. They couldn't afford to eat out, and Sue always stretched the meat for several meals and didn't want to use it all up on making hamburgers.

So, she told her son to ask his Father for what he wanted; she couldn't help him. Her son did pray, and shortly after that a man from their church who worked for a fast food distribution center called to ask if Sue could use some prepackaged hamburgers. The center couldn't distribute them because the package was damaged. Sue said yes, and the man brought over a whole case of them.

One fall, her son decided he wouldn't go to high school because all his pants had holes in them. Again, Sue told him she couldn't afford to buy him new clothes. He would have to ask his Father. Her son prayed again, and a Christian woman from work gave her three bags of nearly new designer clothes for him. He was elated! He had more than enough and gave some of the clothes away.

Sue's daughter wanted to go on a missions trip to Mexico with the youth department one summer. She needed $1,000 to go and had to pay a deposit right away. Sue told her to pray about it. If God wanted her to go, He would provide. Every penny of the money came in by the deadline required. Her daughter went on the trip, and it totally changed her perspective on her own need.

On each of these occasions, Sue and her children learned a little more about trusting God. With God as the head of her family, Sue finally found her "happy" home.

Sue's children are young adults now, building their own lives. Although they've gone through some rough times as a family, her children are Christians and learning to follow the Lord. They are very cautious about serious relationships and they're waiting on God for good marriages.

Although her ex-husband married someone else, Sue is still single, but she's content. She has a good career and a decent home. She's slowly replacing the hand-me-down furniture one piece at a time, when she can afford it. She has credit but she avoids using it. She helped establish a support group for single moms at her church to share the encouragement and hope she received.

A PRINCIPLE TO REMEMBER
Raise your children the way you should have been raised.

"Correct your son, and he will give you comfort; he will also delight your soul" (Proverbs 29:17).

THE UNEXPECTED DIVORCE

It has often been said that it takes two to get a divorce. As many divorced people will attest, that is not always the case in America today. Although it may be true that both spouses had a part in the events leading up to a divorce, quite often the actual divorce is the sole action of one spouse and comes as a shock to the other.

Looking back over the events leading to a divorce, a trained observer might note many signs that indicated one or the other of the spouses was getting ready to split. But unfortunately the unsuspecting party usually doesn't see the signs or refuses to admit that it might happen, especially when both of them are Christians. After all, haven't we been taught that marriage for Christians is for a lifetime?

USING WHAT YOU HAVE

Ann had been married for nearly half of her 46 years to a man who seemed the epitome of stability. Harry owned a computer software company that he and Ann had started 20 years earlier. Ann stopped working in the business when their first child was born 18 years earlier. She continued to do the financial records in their home until their second daughter was born four years later. Then she gradually lost contact with the business.

Harry and Ann were members of a large evangelical church in their community, where Harry served as a deacon. It seemed that their entire lives were built around their church and friends from church. Over the years several of their friends had marital problems, and usually it was Harry and Ann they turned to for help. Several couples in the church publicly stated that they owed their continued marriage to Harry and Ann's counsel and concern.

Harry's business prospered, but it was clear that it would never be a major corporation and Harry would never be an international tycoon. They often had talked about the plans he had when they began the business. He wanted to have a platform to influence people for the Lord and, in fact, had often shared his testimony before business and civic groups in their community.

When Harry turned 45, Ann noticed a change. He often was depressed and moody. Sometimes he refused to get out of bed and seemed indifferent to the children. On occasion they would joke about Harry being in a mid-life crisis. Ann assumed it was a phase he was going through and it would pass.

Then one evening something happened to shake Ann's world. The phone rang. "Is Harry there?" the young female voice on the other end of the line asked.

"Yes, he is," Ann answered. "But he's in the shower right now. Could I help you?"

"No, just tell him Miriam called," the young woman said.

Later, as Harry came into the bedroom, Ann said, "A young woman by the name of Miriam called for you a little earlier. Who is she?"

"Oh, just a girl we're interviewing for a job as a programmer," Harry said in a slightly irritated voice.

Ann let it drop but she thought, *That's strange that someone they interviewed would call here about a job.*

About a week later the phone rang and Ann answered it, "Yes, this is Mrs. Stromm. May I help you?"

"No! Just ask Harry to call me when he comes in, please."

"Who is this?" Ann demanded.

"Harry will know who it is!" she snapped back. "Just tell him to call!" With that the phone went dead.

Ann had a sick feeling that something was definitely wrong. When Harry came home about an hour later, Ann met him at the door. "Harry, I believe that same woman called here again demanding that you call her. Don't tell me she's a prospective employee. What's going on?"

Harry put down his briefcase and said, "I'm leaving, Ann. I just don't love you anymore, and there is someone else."

"Is it that young woman who has been calling here?" Ann asked, as she fought back the tears.

"Yes," Harry replied. "Please don't make a scene, Ann. You must have known our marriage has been over for some time now."

Ann was devastated by Harry's comment. "No, I didn't," she replied. "I knew you were going through some problems, but I didn't think they were about us."

"I just can't stand it here anymore, Ann. You're a good person, probably too good for me. I just need some space. I'll be moving some of my things out tonight. I'll send for the rest of them. Don't worry, you'll be well provided for."

"Is that all I mean to you, Harry—someone you need to provide for? What about our commitment to each other? What about all those other couples you told to stick it out even when they didn't feel like they loved their mate?"

"It just doesn't work for me," Harry said as he headed up the stairs. "I feel more alive when I'm with Miriam than I ever did with you."

As Harry left the room Ann sat down on the couch in shock. She felt like her legs wouldn't hold her up anymore. *What have I done wrong?* she thought, as her mind reeled in panic. *What will I do?*

She began to assume the role that would be hers throughout the separation and ultimate divorce. As she went into the bedroom where Harry was packing his suitcase she pled, "Harry, please don't leave. Whatever I've done to make you feel this way, I know I can change. Don't throw away twenty-five years of marriage. Please!"

"Ann, it just doesn't work anymore. I care about you as a person, but I just don't love you anymore. I need to start a new life and so do you. You'll meet someone who will love you for who you are."

"But tell me what I've done," Ann begged. "I know I can change!"

"You just never allow me to be who I really am," Harry said as he jerked away from her hands. "You strangle me with all this home life stuff. I've still got a life to live and I just need someone who is willing to go with the flow—like Miriam."

For the next several weeks Ann continued to call Harry and apologize for every real and imagined offense she had ever committed. She made the typical mistake that many frightened spouses make of taking on the guilt for Harry's unfaithful actions. The more she pleaded, the more remote Harry became.

"Ann, please stop calling me," Harry said callously over the phone. "I just don't want to live with you anymore. And it won't do any good to send Pastor Reed over here again. He was here yesterday and I told him I'm not subject to his authority. God wants me to be happy. He certainly doesn't want us to be miserable the rest of our lives."

"Are you living with that other woman?" Ann asked in tears.

"Stop torturing yourself, Ann. Yes, we're living together, but we consider ourselves married already. After all, marriage isn't just what's written down on a piece of paper. We're going to be married just as soon as the divorce is final."

As the days went by, Ann found herself unable to get out of bed in the mornings. In spite of herself she found that she was calling Harry and promising him anything if he would just come back. She had stripped away all the veneer of dignity and was actually groveling. Even her closest friend, Mary, tried to bring her back into balance, but Ann was living in fear now and couldn't shake it.

"Ann, you have to snap out of this," Mary told her. "You're not responsible for what Harry's doing. Stop demeaning yourself."

"I can't, Mary. I don't know what I'm going to do. Now Harry is saying that he isn't going to be able to support us after the divorce because the business isn't doing well."

"Well, is it?" Mary asked irritably.

"It was when Harry left. I think it's Miriam's fault. She doesn't want Harry to support us."

"Ann, you need to get a good lawyer to help you make Harry do what's right. His girlfriend knows that you're vulnerable and is taking advantage of you. What has happened to your trust in the Lord, Ann? God hasn't given up on you just because Harry has."

"Oh, Mary," Ann cried, "I don't even know if I believe in God. If there is a God, why would He let this happen to me?"

"I don't know the answer, Ann, except that apparently God never forces any of us to follow Him. Harry had a choice to make and he made it. I know God doesn't like it anymore than you do, but it is Harry's choice. Your choice is whether you're going to make him provide for his family."

"But doesn't God's Word say that I am to honor my husband?"

"Sure it does. Just like it tells Harry to love and cherish you, but Harry chose to divorce you. You at least have the right to defend yourself. You aren't the offending party, Ann. You're the victim."

The next several weeks dragged by as Ann conditioned herself to the fact that Harry wasn't coming back. She would see him driving a new red sports car around town, with that young woman draped all over him. It made her heart ache, but it also helped to strengthen her.

Then one day she discovered that she didn't feel quite so depressed anymore. She actually felt like getting up and helping the girls clean the house. *All this time,* she thought, *I've been so wrapped up in my pity that I haven't thought about the girls' feelings.*

That morning she asked, "Carrie, Kristy, what do you girls think about what's happening to Dad and me?"

"Mom," Kristy, the youngest, said, "If I were you, I'd go over to his condo and slash the tires on his little car. He never bought you a new sports car, and you stuck it out during the bad times."

Carrie then said, "Mom, Dad told me he wasn't going to be able to help me with college. It's like he doesn't want us to be his family anymore. That girlfriend of his is not much older than I am."

"Girls, I don't want you to hate your father. I don't understand why he's doing this, but we just have to learn to live with it and get on with our lives."

"Mom, he's going to try to cut out on you and leave you with nothing. You can't let him do that. Mary's right. You have to fight him."

"I can't do that, girls. Just because he doesn't love us anymore doesn't mean we can't love him. If I fight, the court battle will be nasty and expensive. I believe we have to turn Dad over to the Lord and accept that God is still in control. If so, He won't let us down."

"Oh get real, Mom," Kristy said with a roll of her eyes. "Dad's having the time of his life and we're barely scraping by now. Do you think he's going to care that you'll be broke? He'll just buy another sports car to celebrate."

"Mrs. Stromm, I have no alternative but to grant your husband's divorce decree, according to the laws of our state," the judge said in response to her plea against the divorce hearing. "He cites irreconcilable differences and has waited the prescribed amount of time."

Ann was crushed again. *It seems like every time I begin to feel normal again something else happens,* Ann thought as her attorney put his arm around her. She had hoped that Harry would snap out of whatever he was going through now that his girlfriend had left. Instead he seemed to withdraw even further. It was like he had lost all confidence in himself. She had even heard that the business was going downhill because of neglect. She walked out of the courtroom single again—after all these years.

She was feeling that old panic that had ruled her life in the early stages of their separation. *What will I do?* She asked herself silently. *I haven't held a job outside my home for twenty years.* She looked at herself in the car mirror. "Well Ann," she said aloud, "I guess it's time to get realistic. Harry doesn't want you anymore. All you have left is your girls."

"And God," a little voice said somewhere inside her mind.

The next few weeks were spent searching the want ads for jobs for which she might be qualified. Once, she even went so far as to apply for a position as a night waitress at a new restaurant. But when the manager had said, "I'm sorry, lady, but we're really looking for someone with experience," she had retreated back to her home, defeated and depressed. "I can't even get a job as a waitress," Ann said to her friend Mary.

"Do you want a job as a waitress, Ann?" Mary asked very matter-of-factly.

"I don't know what I want to do. I've been a housewife and that's what I enjoy. I like being with my children and maintaining a home."

"But haven't you worked on some committees and helped to organize several political rallies? If I remember right, you were pretty good at organizing and getting other people involved."

"Oh sure," Ann said as she poured herself another cup of coffee, "and there's a lot of demand for a middle-aged housewife to organize parties and rallies I guess!"

"Who knows? There might be. Have you ever thought about starting a small party catering service out of your home? I'll bet there are a lot of working mothers who would hire you to plan birthday parties and maybe even some businesses that would want to have meetings catered."

Ann stopped and considered what Mary said. "You know, you just might be right. But how would I go about finding them?"

"Why don't you talk with Pastor Reed and see if he would let you put a note on the church bulletin board? We have a pretty large church. I'll bet you would get some response."

That week Ann went to see the pastor about posting a notice on the bulletin board. "Ann, I think it's a good idea. You really do have a gift of organization. I think you would do well with a catering business. You need to check on the necessary permits and licenses first though."

"Permits and licenses?" Ann asked in a puzzled tone. "I didn't even think about that. What would they cost?"

"I don't really know, Ann. But I would imagine they're not too expensive. I'll call Bill Moore, one of our members who's an attorney, and see if he can give you some help."

"That's kind of you, Pastor, but I don't want to be a burden to anyone."

"Ann, you need to realize that you're not a burden. We're your family and we want to help you if you'll let us. It seems like you have shut the church out since you and Harry started having problems."

"I guess I felt like I didn't deserve to be a part of the church, Pastor. I know divorce is a sin, and I wasn't even sure that I believed in God anymore."

"What you are feeling isn't unusual, Ann. Most people feel that way about a divorce. In many ways a divorce is worse than a death, because the hurt often runs deeper. More often than not, the injured party takes on all the guilt. With the death of a spouse, the hurt lessens over time; but, in a divorce, the hurt remains because the ex-partner is still around."

"I can't seem to let go, Pastor Reed," Ann said. "I know Harry doesn't love me anymore, but I still love him."

"Ann, I doubt that Harry even knows what he wants or doesn't want right now. I tried to talk to him several times, but he won't listen. He keeps saying that God wants him to be happy. Right now he thinks being happy means being totally free to do whatever he wants. Nobody is that free, and eventually Harry will realize that. Don't give up hope. God is still in charge and when Harry is willing to listen, God will speak the truth in his ear."

"I don't know, Pastor. He acts like he doesn't care about his family at all."

"Ann, Harry is going through what I've heard called the mid-life crisis. It's something a lot of men experience in their 40s or 50s. They're trying to recapture their youth. One day he'll wake up and realize that he's being stupid. If you're open, he may even try to ask for your help. In the meantime you just need to get on with your life and let God do whatever has to be done in Harry's life."

"I'll certainly try, Pastor. But right now I feel like I need to get busy. Harry's business is failing and he's not sending us enough to live on."

After she applied for the proper licenses and permits, Ann posted her notice on the church's bulletin board. Her first client was the attorney who helped her. He asked her to cater an office party for a senior partner who was retiring. The party was a huge success, and Ann's business was launched. Within six months she had three part-time people working for her and was booked up several weeks in advance.

She heard from several people at church that Harry's business continued to decline and that he had lost his biggest customer due to an equipment breakdown that had delayed a vital software package from being completed on time. Ann's business still wasn't generating enough income to support her and the girls, but the trend was improving monthly.

* * * * * * * * * * * *

Ann became a success story. She was one of the fortunate few divorced women who was able to generate most of her income needs without struggling in the job market. However, most women in Ann's situation find themselves in desperate straits financially and in need of outside help just to make ends meet. The resources needed are readily available within most local churches.

The unfortunate truth is that most Christians have been blinded to the needs of single parents. They somehow think that the government provides all their needs. Not so. Single parents don't need welfare; they need friends who care. The only long-term solution to the dilemma of single parents is a good job with adequate pay.

That means facing the job market, but we'll talk about that later in the book.

A PRINCIPLE TO REMEMBER
God provides for those who are faithful.

"Offer to God a sacrifice of thanksgiving, and pay your vows to the Most High; and call upon Me in the day of trouble; I shall rescue you, and you will honor Me" (Psalm 50:14-15).

Chapter 3

THE NEVER MARRIED PARENT

It saddens me to recognize that this chapter needs to be included, but the statistics cannot be ignored. As mentioned earlier, 38 percent of all children born in single parent families are born to unwed parents. Most of these children are fatherless, and most of these families are poor. Many people believe these parents are just victims of an immoral society; others say the government is perpetuating the problem; still others blame the pro-life movement. Who is to blame is not really the issue. The fact is, never-married parents are a reality, and they need God's love and the church's help.

It may surprise you to know that the average age of an unwed mother is about 20 and the father is 25 or 26. Teen pregnancy is decreasing, due partly to extensive abstinence campaigns started by Christians. In addition, many more single career women are choosing to parent children alone, either through artificial insemination or brief affairs. These women often don't want a committed relationship with the father; they just want to have a baby before they are too old, and they want to have the experience of giving birth rather than adopting.

Some respected Christian women are adopting children to raise alone. Although I appreciate their love and compassion for needy children, I wonder at their belief that they can provide balanced stability alone. They need to have a tremendous support system in place to take on such a responsibility.

SARA'S STORY

Sara came from a Christian home. Both of her parents attended church regularly. So did Sara and her sister. Sara grew up in church and was involved in the children's and youth programs. Her dad worked and traveled a lot. Her mom was active in the women's ministry and volunteered a lot at church. Sara's sister Tracy was the perfect child. She earned good grades and never made any trouble for their parents.

Sara was the strong-willed one and had a hard time being obedient. She had to work extra hard to gain her parents' attention. However, she never considered herself a "bad" girl, and she would never do anything that would hurt her parents.

Like most teens, she started judging her appearance and home life by those around her. Even though Sara was very attractive and had an outgoing personality that attracted people to her easily, she began to feel like she didn't fit in. She went to a public school and found it more and more difficult to be different—to be a Christian. She spent much of her time dancing with her friends. She really liked dancing and apparently she was pretty good, because she always received a lot of attention from the boys.

Sara thought Scott was the cutest boy in school, and he swept her off her feet when she was 17. When they started dating, her parents were very concerned that Scott didn't attend church anywhere. Sara assured them that he was a Christian and his parents attended another church. He usually missed church because of football practice and games the day before.

Sara and Scott both decided they wanted to wait until marriage for sex. Sara was confident that their passionate petting would always stop before it was too late. After all, Scott respected her. Sara remained confident until another girl caught Scott's attention, but then she immediately felt threatened and feared she would lose Scott.

The next time they were together Sara allowed their passion to overtake them. She reasoned that if she gave herself to the man she loved this would seal their relationship, and Scott wouldn't look at another girl. It worked for a few months, then Scott wanted to break it off because of his interest in the other girl. Sara was crushed. Soon after that, she found out she was pregnant.

Sara didn't know how to tell her mom and dad. She had just turned 18 and was supposed to start college in the fall. She had planned and dreamed about her career most of her life. She knew she wanted to be a television news anchor. She tried to talk to Scott, but he denied fathering her child! She couldn't believe it! He said if she would sleep with him, how did he know she wouldn't sleep with others. Besides, he didn't love her anymore, and there was someone else in his life.

After trying to talk to Scott on several more occasions, Sara finally realized he was not going to go through this with her. She braced herself and waited for the best time to talk to her mother. Naturally, her mother's reaction was shock and hurt, and she began to cry.

Sara's mom's first concern was how she would break the news to Sara's dad, and then she wondered how the people at church would react when they heard the news. She didn't understand how Sara could do this to them.

Then she became angry and, speaking from her anger, she starting saying how she wished the whole thing had never happened and she wanted the whole thing to go away.

Sara couldn't believe it! "Mom, you aren't thinking that I should have an abortion?"

"No, no, you can't do that. We're Christians!" her mother said, secretly wishing they could. Then she came up with a solution. "We could send you on a long trip. We could say you went away to school. You could have the baby and come back and no one would ever know."

"I would know!" shouted Sara. "I'm not giving up my baby! I've already lost the man I love. Now you're asking me to give up my baby! Would you give up your baby?" She broke down in uncontrollable sobs.

Her mother suddenly realized how she must have sounded. She hugged her daughter and told Sara that she just needed time to deal with her own feelings. She was afraid, hurt, and angry, and she just couldn't deal with Sara's feelings right now.

"We'll just wait till your father gets home. He'll know what to do," her mother reasoned. It was all the comfort she could give at the moment.

When Sara's father came home, they told him about the baby. Understandably, he was very upset; however, he reacted differently and focused on Sara's feelings. He wanted to protect her and make things right. His first response was to kill Scott. Then he wanted a shotgun wedding. Finally, he realized his little girl was probably on her own.

The family decided that Sara would stay with them until the baby was born. After that she would have to move out. They were not ready to raise another child. Sara was an adult and she had to deal with her decision to get pregnant.

During her pregnancy, Sara repented and cried continuously. She was very scared. She prayed God would not allow her baby to pay for her sins.

When Sara's pastor heard about the baby, she was called into counseling. He asked if she had repented, and she assured him she had. He asked if she was going to abstain from sexual activity. Again she said yes. He asked about the father, and she told what she knew about him and how he had reacted. Then the pastor prayed for her. Later the church gave Sara a baby shower. The gifts from the many who came were a tremendous blessing.

Matthew came into the world early on a Saturday morning in March. He was the picture of health. Sara's parents were typical grandparents, doting over little Matt, but they stuck by their decision. Sara would have to move out as soon as possible.

She filed paternity papers on Scott, who had gone away to college. His parents wouldn't tell her where he went; his friends wouldn't tell either. For now, it would be just Sara and Matt.

She applied for government assistance and looked for a place to live. All she could find was a little upstairs efficiency apartment in a dilapidated old house. It wasn't in a very good neighborhood, but it was all she could afford. She had wanted subsidized housing, but she would have to wait; there were no more units available.

She searched for as many community resources as she could to keep Matt heathy. She found formula and medical assistance. That would have to do.

Her parents told everyone at church that Sara had moved out, but they didn't say where she lived. They were concerned about the location where she was living and also the condition of the place, and they told Sara it was not a good choice. They thought that since she was receiving government assistance she could make a better choice. Plus, they were helping out now and then with groceries and rent.

Sara took Matt for walks almost every day. She wasn't one who could sit still for very long. After a few weeks, she began to feel like she knew the neighborhood and was beginning to feel safe. Then one afternoon she started out the door with Matt and something startled her. She felt like someone was watching her; it was an eerie feeling. She almost headed back in the door but thought it was just her imagination and went on.

She was halfway down the street and the feeling just wouldn't go away. She kept turning back to look, but she didn't see anything. Suddenly, someone jumped out of nowhere and grabbed her from behind by the throat. She struggled to see who her attacker was and tried to scream. She tried to break free, but it was no use. He must have been a strong man because she couldn't move. Couldn't he see she had a baby in her arms? Little Matt began to wail.

The attacker stopped for a second, then shoved little Matt to the ground. She was terrified! She didn't breathe. She just waited. Was Matt okay? After a few seconds, Matt began to wail again. *At least he's alive,* she thought. Then she was shoved to the ground too. *This is it,* she thought, *I'm going to die right here on the sidewalk. Don't the neighbors hear Matt crying? Can't anyone see what's happening? Why doesn't someone help me?*

The attacker pushed himself on top of her and started tearing at her clothes. She realized he had a hat pulled down over most of his face, and he had a knife. She stopped struggling for a second, took a deep breath, and prayed, "Dear God, show me how to get out of this! Please help me and Matt!" Then she reached out to feel for anything she could use as a weapon that might have fallen out of her purse. Yes! She found her keys, grabbed them, and shoved them as hard as she could into the attacker's eyes.

In the seconds it took for him to respond to the pain and realize what was happening, Sara had shoved him off. She grabbed Matt and began to run. The attacker was on his feet and after her. She ran into a house through an unlatched screen door. The startled residents gaped as Sara slammed the storm door and locked it. After she told them what had happened, they let her call the police. She was safe. She knew God had spared them.

The police took Sara and Matt to the hospital to see if they were okay and called Sara's parents and pastor. Sara had a small cut on her throat where the attacker held the knife. She was bruised and shaken but all right. Little Matt was bleeding on the side of his head from hitting the pavement. They would need to keep him under observation to be sure there was no internal bleeding or a concussion. When the pastor and her parents arrived and heard what Sara and Matt had been through, they agreed Sara would have to move.

With the church finally knowing the whole situation, they could help Sara. They temporarily moved her in with another family in the church while they counseled Sara and her parents. They helped Sara plan for the college education she needed to enable her to take care of Matt and herself. They convinced her parents to allow Sara to live with them until she finished school. And they helped her locate Scott so the paternity tests could be done.

Matt was three years old before Sara ever received support from Scott. He still hadn't seen his son. She'd heard he was married.

Sara graduated with an associate degree in communications and, through friends from the church, landed an entry level job at a local television station. She started working with a budget counselor as soon as she started receiving pay checks. She began dating a wonderful man from church, and after a while they set a wedding date.

It's unfortunate that shame or pride keeps us from sharing our concerns with others. Sara might never have had to go through that traumatic experience if she or her parents had talked to the church first. It was a loving church that offered all they could to help someone in need. Not every church will respond to an unwed mother like Sara's did, but isn't it worth the risk to find out, instead of trying to go it alone?

The church is becoming more aware of the needs of the unwed mother as more and more are choosing to have their babies, rather than abort them. They are recognizing the need for ongoing support if these families are ever going to become productive and healed.

A PRINCIPLE TO REMEMBER
Don't be too quick to judge what others have done.

"Do not judge lest you be judged. For in the way you judge, you will be judged; and by your standard of measure, it will be measured to you" (Matthew 7:1-2).

CUSTODIAL FATHERS

ingle fathering is not a new phenomenon. In earlier eras it was the father who was usually left to raise the children alone, even if a divorce was involved. This was primarily due to the father's resources. Women usually did not have resources of their own. All of that changed during World War II, when women proved they could work and provide for their families. If they couldn't, the government stepped in with support. In many cases, the father was no longer necessary as the sole provider.

Over the years, women's fight for independence brought them much favor and support in the courtroom, but some unexpected consequences developed. Many women who believed they could have it all—things, money, husband, career, and children—began to realize they had been deceived. Divorce and unwed pregnancies began to rise dramatically.

Although women gained favor in the courts because they were supposed to be able to care for themselves, monetary support from former spouses began to decrease dramatically. More and more women became dependent on the government. In 1994 almost 90 percent of the poor receiving aid were single-mother families.

The government began to pressure the courts for more support and involvement from the fathers. The courts began rethinking the role of the father as provider, and today there is an increased demand for the father's support for his family, and there are a growing number of custodial single fathers. However, most of them don't have the overwhelming financial concerns of a custodial single mother. Their needs are more social in nature.

Patrick Batchelder, editor of the *Dear Dad* newsletter, has been a full-time custodial father for many years. He began raising his son and daughter when they were just infants. Most of the people he met when he was out with his kids didn't realize he was a single dad; they thought he was just giving mom a break.

He found that the church really didn't know how to respond to him. He was brought casserole dinners and invited to singles groups, when what he really needed was for him and his children to be accepted as a family. He didn't have time to do "singles" things. His time focused on providing and caring for his children.

Patrick says fathers are already trained to handle problems and provide for their families; they don't need to be taught that. They need to spend time together as a family and spend time with other families. His *Dear Dad* newsletter focuses on the single fathers and how they can develop the qualities needed to parent successfully alone. (If you are interested in the *Dear Dad* newsletter, call 1-800-Dear-Dad.)

JASON'S STORY

Although most custodial dads are able to provide adequately for their families, many struggle financially. Jason's situation is a good example. Although he was raised in church and knew right from wrong, Jason was barely 17 years old when he became a single father. Jason was good-looking with a likeable, somewhat sheepish personality, and he had a lot going for him. He displayed a lot of artistic talent and planned a career in graphic arts.

Because of his all-American good looks, Jason did a little modeling and met a lot of attractive girls. Even with all the attention, his self-image was not what it should've been. He seemed to have a deep need to be loved and accepted. When Jill, a particularly attractive older girl, began to notice him, he discovered it felt good to be the object of her attention. The relationship was intense, and because Jill was experienced sexually, the relationship escalated quickly. However, it ended just as quickly when Jason found out Jill also was having a sexual relationship with someone else.

A few weeks after the breakup, Jill told Jason she was pregnant. He didn't believe her, because he thought they were "careful." Eventually, he could see that it was true. She insisted he was the father; but, with his knowledge about the other relationship, he didn't believe her and insisted on paternity testing.

A year after a baby girl was born, Jason learned that he really was the baby's father. He felt terrible that he had missed a year of his little Chelsea's life. Even though he was still living at home and attending high school, he immediately became involved with his daughter. He had no income to support her, so he began working part-time. Child support was mounting even though he paid what he could.

Chelsea got to know her daddy and his family during the alternating weekend visits. When Jason graduated from high school he worked full-time until he could get into graphic design school. He was able to catch up on some of the past-due child support. He began college the next fall and continued working as many hours as he could. Jill began to date other men and left Chelsea with her parents a lot, and although Jason was able to see her more, he was increasingly concerned about Jill leaving her so much. He sought custody but was turned down. Even though Jill was on public assistance, he couldn't prove that he could provide for her any better. He would either have to prove that Jill was an unfit mother or wait until he could provide for his daughter to try for custody again.

The strain of living with his parents began to take its toll. His schedule didn't match theirs, and when he brought Chelsea home the family had to pitch in a lot. Although they adored Chelsea, his mom and dad found the unpredictability of her visits very hard to deal with. She had two sets of rules and two ways of doing almost everything.

Jason's mom made sure he was the one to put Chelsea to bed, change her, feed her, play with her, and be there for her. But, the financial burdens fell mostly on his parents while Jason was attending school. Although his parents were very supportive, Jason knew he would have to move out eventually, but he didn't know how he was going to make it.

After two years, Jason graduated from graphic arts school and landed an entry level job at an advertising firm. Jill took off for another state with a new boyfriend and took Chelsea with her. Jason found them and brought Chelsea back home. He found out when Jill returned home that she was pregnant again by the new boyfriend. He went back to court for custody, and this time the court decided in his favor.

Jason moved out of his parent's home and into a small apartment. He bought a used car on credit to get back and forth to work; his parents gave him the down payment. By the time he paid for rent and child care, his entry level income was almost gone.

Chelsea got sick and Jason took a couple of days off to care for her. When he returned to work he was let go; they needed someone who could be there. He knew he couldn't move back in with his parents. He felt like he already had drained them financially and emotionally. So he took a job in another city and tried again to support his daughter.

Jason's pay was higher with the new job, and he figured he would have enough. But the demands of raising a child were still too much to handle alone. For the first few months he had to pay all their medical expenses until they were covered by insurance. He no longer had his family's financial or physical support, and Chelsea needed so much he couldn't give her. He tried to make up for her lack through adventurous outings and new toys, but he was just getting deeper in debt.

He had to be at work every day or he would lose his job again, so he had to pay extra for someone to keep Chelsea when she was sick. Although Jason was attending church occasionally, he didn't share any of his concerns with anyone there. Men were not supposed to be needy.

He met a young lady at church who was drawn to him. Many women are drawn to nurturing men. Amy seemed to be pretty stable, and she adored Chelsea. Jason and Amy were just good friends; then they started dating. Jason had broken the barrier of abstinence in his last relationship, and he and Amy quickly crossed the line into intimacy. He had failed again.

Jason knew they couldn't take back what they'd done. He had really grown to love Amy and wanted to commit to her, but he was afraid to trust again and needed more time. They decided they would try to control their passions, but they soon discovered she was already pregnant.

The situation was rocky from the beginning. They told their parents they planned to get married as soon as possible, but they had a big stumbling block. Jason's insurance wouldn't cover the prenatal care or delivery. Amy's parents were understandably upset and wanted her to stay home with them and have nothing more to do with Jason. When her parents found out their insurance wouldn't cover the expenses either, Amy signed up for welfare benefits.

Jason's parents wished they could wash their hands of the whole mess. Once was hard enough, but twice was ridiculous. They couldn't understand their son's behavior. They loved him and they couldn't really reject him or the children, but they wouldn't let him move back home. Jason needed to take responsibility for his behavior. So, this time he moved in with his sister and brother-in-law and their children.

As soon as he could, Jason got a new job and moved out on his own again. A baby girl was born, and Jason and Amy got married. With everything looking more legitimate, the families became more involved. For a time everything seemed to be working out. He was starting to pay off their debts and had someone there for his children. He was in love and happy with his life.

About a year after his second daughter, Jamie, was born, his wife told him their marriage wasn't working. She was too young to be tied down with two children and she wanted to be free. She was leaving and she was taking Jamie with her. Apparently, she had become involved with someone else, so she filed for divorce and moved out.

Jason was devastated. He didn't know how he would go through this again. He had thoughts of suicide and suffered deep depression. He knew his girls needed him, but he just couldn't find the strength to be there for them. His family didn't think he should be alone, so he moved back in with his sister. She helped him care for Chelsea while he tried to reassemble his life.

Jason turned to God in his despair and began to attend church to fill his overwhelming void; he needed it and so did Chelsea. He attended a divorce recovery group, and his emotions began to heal.

His parents attended a financial planning seminar and started working with Jason on his budget—that way they would know his financial situation and when he really needed help. His sister began to let go of some of the responsibility for Chelsea's care as soon as Jason was able to take on more.

Jason probably will have to live with his sister and her family for a while. Both families are working to become debt free and his sister and brother-in-law are considering purchasing a larger home in the future, where Jason and his children would be welcome to stay. Jamie visits every other weekend. Jason's parents watch all the grandchildren one evening every other weekend so Jason and his sister and brother-in-law can have a break.

Jamie's mother, Amy, is engaged to be married, and since she's starting a new family Jason would like to have both of his girls grow up together, so he hopes to get custody of Jamie too.

* * * * * * * * * * * *

Even though he has a supportive Christian family to lean on, Jason's future will not be easy. He has some consequences he may have to live with for a long time. We often think our actions don't affect anyone but ourselves; but, as we can see from Jason's life, our actions have repercussions on everyone around us. Jason has taken some positive steps that will make restoration a lot more likely.

Often the church and the parents have to deal with situations like this after the fact. Even if Jason had gone to the church with his need, they might not have known how to help him. He admits that he really didn't think about or know what he was getting into at age 16, even though he'd had sex education in school.

He believes that it may have made a difference if the church had taught about the real consequences of premarital sex. They did teach that premarital sex was sin. But he, and many of his Christian friends, believed the prominent cultural lie from movies, television, and school: that it was just a natural part of growing up. If he was "in love" and committed to the girl, it was okay. No one talked about the possibility, responsibility, or struggles of single parenting.

Since most churches don't address the issue before a crisis pregnancy happens, they at least need to be prepared to deal with these situations after the fact. These young parents need to come to repentance. And they need healing: physically, emotionally, and spiritually.

Often young people do not have the support of their families in these situations. They need someone to help them understand their responsibilities to God, to their children, to the other parent, and to themselves. They need help understanding finances and developing a practical budget.

Young men like Jason need relationships with stable couples to establish models for their children. Also, they need to know that someone cares for them and that they can learn to handle things differently.

A PRINCIPLE TO REMEMBER
God uses people to help people.

"At this present time your abundance being a supply for their want, that their abundance also may become a supply for your want, that there may be equality" (2 Corinthians 8:14).

Chapter 5

LOSING A SPOUSE

Dealing with the death of a spouse is difficult—both emotionally and financially. At a time when adjusting is most difficult, multiple decisions are thrust upon the grieving spouse. Nearly 80 percent of all surviving spouses are women. A common factor among most of the widows I have counseled was the lack of good, unbiased counsel available to them.

The majority of widows do not have large amounts of money available to them. Typically their husbands were employed in average income jobs, had a nominal amount of insurance ($25,000 to $50,000) and practically no assets, except a home with a mortgage and a car with more debt than equity. Many widows end up depending on Social Security and, if they still have children to raise, on dependent care benefits. These single parents often are forced into the workplace, and any insurance money they received is used as a buffer until the children are grown. Generally they have a difficult time.

Eighty percent of the widows under the age of 50 will remarry within five years, creating a whole new set of decisions and possible conflicts. Should she have a prenuptial agreement for the funds from her first marriage? What if her husband has children too? Should her children's monthly benefits be held only for their care? These and many other related questions can best be answered on the basis of

God's Word. But I'm getting ahead of myself. First, let's consider widows without assets.

THE CASE OF STACY

Stacy was 32 years old when her husband Tom first learned that he had cancer. Over the next two years they spent hundreds of thousands of dollars on medical treatments. Fortunately Tom had good insurance through his employer but, even so, they still had to pay the 20 percent deductible, up to $10,000 each year. This effectively depleted their reserves and forced them to sell their home for the equity.

When Tom died, two years after being diagnosed, they were down to living paycheck to paycheck. They had been members of a large Baptist church for several years and had many friends there who helped during the last dark hours when Tom was wasting away. They brought meals to the family, and in the last few weeks several of the older ladies sat with Tom at the hospital in the evenings so that Stacy could get some rest.

During that time several people asked Stacy about their finances but, in typical fashion for most people, she always responded, "We're making it okay." Usually that's where they left it after saying, "Well if you ever have a need, you call us." That's a pretty safe statement in our generation, because our inherent pride will keep most of us from asking. It is only by consistent prodding that these barriers are broken down. It's not that most Christians don't care; they do. But they also don't want to feel pushy.

Tom had a total of $10,000 in life insurance. He had known that he needed more, but funds were always tight, and it wasn't a high priority for a man under 30. After he was diagnosed with cancer he was totally uninsurable. Guilt kept him from discussing it with Stacy, even though they both knew she would have a difficult time financially trying to support their three children after his death.

The insurance proceeds were sent almost immediately after the company received the death certificate from their insurance agent. Stacy paid the funeral bill of nearly $2,500 and some miscellaneous outstanding bills amounting to $1,200. She then deposited the remainder in her savings account to live on while Social Security processed her application for benefits.

Several weeks went by with no word from Social Security, during which time Stacy called the local office several times. All she could find out was that the claim had been filed and forwarded to the Washington office. Stacy then wrote a letter to the national headquarters, telling them of her urgency.

A few days later she received a letter from the Social Security administration, stating that there was a problem with her claim and giving her a number to call for further information. When she called the number she told the receptionist her name and was asked to hold on while her call was being transferred to a claims worker.

"Hello, Mrs. Johnston?" the case worker asked.

"Yes, this is Mrs. Johnston," Stacy replied.

"Mrs. Johnston, we seem to have a problem with your application for Social Security survivor benefits."

"What kind of problem?" Stacy asked. She could sense her heart speeding up in response to the comment.

"It seems that our records of your husband, Thomas, only go back to 1983. Did he work at a job that was exempt from Social Security assessment before that?"

"Why no, I'm sure he didn't. We've been married nearly 10 years now and Tom worked for two other firms, but they all paid into Social Security."

"There must be some kind of mix-up in the records then," the case worker said. "Have you ever requested an audit of your husband's Social Security account?"

"No, I didn't know I could."

"Yes, it's a service provided by the department. Unfortunately we aren't required to adjust any file beyond three years if a discrepancy occurs."

"What exactly does that mean?" Stacy asked as her anxiety level heightened more.

"It means, since your husband's account shows contributions only since 1983, your benefits will be greatly reduced."

Panic struck. "That simply can't be!" Stacy said desperately. "Tom paid in all those years, even before we were married. What can I do to get this straightened out?"

"I would suggest you write a letter to the district supervisor. Do you have any employment records for the years prior to 1983?"

"I'm not sure. Tom kept all the records."

"Well it might help if you had some evidence. You can get a copy of your income tax statements from the Internal Revenue Service. Although sometimes it takes several months to get the copies."

Several months, Stacy thought to herself. *I don't have enough money to last several months.*

After hanging up the phone Stacy ran to the basement to search the old file cabinet where Tom always kept their previous years' records. There, neatly labeled and banded with rubber bands, she found all the income tax statements dating back 15 years.

Praise the Lord for Tom, she thought as she looked over the records. Every withholding statement was attached and all of them reflected Social Security withholding for each year.

Stacy hurried to the local library where she made copies of all the withholding statements. She then wrote a letter to the Social Security district office, as instructed earlier. She mailed the letter the next morning and followed it up with a telephone call as soon as she thought enough time had passed for the letter to arrive.

"Mrs. Johnston, this is Mrs. Combs, the district supervisor for claims. We did receive your letter and the verification of Social Security withholding on your husband, Thomas. I will forward your request for reevaluation to our national office."

"You mean you can't approve my support?" Stacy said as she felt the fear rise again.

"No, I'm afraid not, Mrs. Johnston. That can only be done at the Social Security headquarters. By law, we are not bound to make adjustments after three years."

"But how can you do that?" Stacy cried. "We paid into the system all those years."

"I understand how you feel, Mrs. Johnston. But we didn't make the laws; Congress did. You'll have to wait until your appeal is heard."

Needless to say, Stacy spent some sleepless nights waiting for a reply from the Social Security administration. In the meantime an attorney from her church called their congressman about Stacy's case. The congressman then called the Social Security office to check on her request. He was assured the department would do all they could to rectify the problem.

During this period Stacy discovered what Christian love is all about. When the members of the Sunday school class heard about her dilemma they took up a special offering to help her financially. The next four months she received anonymous gifts totaling nearly $3,000. The church was considering taking the family on as a missions project when she finally got a letter from Social Security.

Dear Mrs. Johnston:
Your request for reevaluation of Social Security survivor's benefits has been received and I'm glad to tell you that the benefits have been recalculated, based on the records you provided. Enclosed is a check for the entire period during which you and your children were entitled.

Fortunately for Stacy and her children she was supported by a strong church family that was willing to obey God's Word. It says, *"What use is it, my brethren, if a man says he has faith, but he has no works? Can that faith save him? If a brother or sister is without clothing and in need of daily food, and one of you says to them, 'Go in peace, be warmed and be filled,' and yet you do not give them what is necessary for their body, what use is that?"* (James 2:14-16).

Stacy's life since she has been widowed has not been easy. But it would have been a much smoother transition if her husband had decided to provide his family with enough insurance to meet their needs for at least a reasonable time period. Obviously God still provided, but I question if it was His best plan.

WIDOWS NEED HELP

Jeffrey and Sheila were happily married for 23 years. With children ages 17, 19, and 22, they realized their nest soon would be empty and they would have the opportunity to start life all over again as a couple. There was an air of excitement as they discussed future plans for just the two of them.

Both were committed Christians who had served as full-time missionaries during the first nine years of their marriage. They lived in severe and stressful conditions in the mission field, so when they left they decided to settle down in a small town in Vermont for mental and emotional rest and spiritual renewal.

Jeffrey began working for a major manufacturing company in the accounting department. As a hobby, he had learned to fly small single-engine planes and shared his passion with anyone who would listen. Flying was a dream come true for Jeffrey. Sheila had never seen him so happy. Although she was happy to see his dreams fulfilled, she did not share his love for airplanes, particularly single-engine planes. She always felt tense and insecure while in the air and couldn't relax until both feet were planted securely on the ground. She once told Jeffrey, "It's not dying I'm afraid of—it's knowing the plane might crash!"

When his boss discovered Jeffrey's interest in flying, he took him aside and made a proposal. "Jeffrey, the company will put you through training to become a certified flight instructor—if you will teach me how to fly."

Jeffrey was thrilled at the prospect of being a corporate pilot. But he had one condition for accepting the job: the company would have to provide life insurance in case of death. The boss met his condition through the company's health insurance. However, it was not enough to provide for a wife and children, so Jeffrey bought extra life insurance.

For years, Jeffrey and Sheila talked openly in their family about their eventual deaths. They had written a letter to the children telling them where to locate their wills and life insurance policies. Down deep, Sheila had thought that she would be the one to go first. But at 44 years of age, she felt death was still at least forty years from becoming a reality.

Sheila had a good job, working for a Christian boss. Most of her coworkers were Christians, and she enjoyed the daily fellowship. It was not unusual for Jeffrey to call during the day to say hello. Consequently, she thought nothing of it when he called one particular wintery day. He joked with her and told her he was flying with his boss to Newport and would be home around 7:30 that evening.

Spenser, their oldest son, was in field training at an Army base in Louisiana. Their daughter Brianne was spending the weekend with her cousin sixty miles away. Sheila and her youngest son, Craig, decided to relax at home and wait for Jeffrey.

Later that day, the cold, snowy weather had produced a thick haze over their county. When Jeffrey didn't return by nine o'clock, Sheila figured he was held up by the weather. She wasn't alarmed because she knew he was a cautious pilot. Her son Craig wanted more than anything to be like his dad and shared his passion for flying. However, that night he began pacing the floor. "Dad can't land at this airport, Mom; the ceiling is too low!"

At 9:45 the phone rang. It was Jeffrey's boss' daughter, sounding very upset. "Sheila, have you heard that there was a plane crash here tonight? Two people were killed. They said the bodies were burned and can't be identified. I'm worried that it's your dad."

Sheila's heart sank as she hung up and looked at her son. He could see that something was wrong. She hugged Craig as she uttered the unspeakable, "There was a crash." She composed herself and tried to comfort herself as well as Craig by adding, "We don't know for sure it was Dad."

Her mind immediately raced as she hurried to change out of her robe. "I've got to call the pastor. I've got to get to the airport. How am I going to tell Spenser and Brianne? How are they going to get home?" She called the pastor and headed for the airport. She had decided not to tell her other children until she knew something for sure.

Later that night, at the small county airport, Sheila and Craig were told the heart-wrenching news: Jeffrey's I.D. bracelet had been found in the wreckage, along with some papers that had survived the fire. Tears wouldn't come for Sheila; there were only deep groans of grief and pain.

Time seemed to stand still as Sheila numbly climbed into the pastor's car to make the trip back home. Her mind continued to race. Should she call the Red Cross? Would they be able to reach Spenser? How would they tell him? She wished she could be with him. Would they bring him home? What about Brianne? She couldn't be told over the phone that her father was killed in a plane crash. Somebody will have to go tell her—and bring her home.

As the pastor and his wife drove them up the driveway to their home, Sheila looked at her house and began to panic. Who's going to take care of everything—the house, the car? Who will take care of the lawn? Jeffrey was a jack-of-all-trades and saved the family a lot of money by doing his own house repairs. Neither of the boys were gifted in that area.

As Sheila tried to sort through what had just happened, and all that needed to be done over the next few days, it hit her with a sickening blow: I'm a *widow!* Coupled with the state of shock that had come over her, she suddenly realized her life was taking a drastic turn. Jeffrey never would come home again.

At 2:00 A.M., two officers from the Sheriff's Department were standing at Sheila's door. "Ma'am, we hate to put you through this tonight, but to positively identify your husband's body, we need to ask some questions." She tried not to think about why they were asking.

The questions were awful, and she answered automatically as she fought the horror she was imagining. "What size shoes did your husband wear? Can you describe what he was wearing today? Was he wearing a wedding band? Were his log books with him on the plane? Did he have any major deformities? Where can we get his dental records?"

A close family friend drove the distance to tell Brianne about her dad and bring her home. The Red Cross was contacted and Spenser was home by 9:30 the next morning. Sheila's church stepped in and took over. Friends and church members started coming in by midnight, bringing abundant food and comfort to Sheila and Craig. The ladies from church cleaned the house. People offered their homes for family members who would be coming in from out of town.

Supernatural strength and energy carried Sheila through the next three days. There was so much that had to be done. Funeral arrangements had to be made. Sheila couldn't help thinking about the fact that Jeffrey had been burned and they could not view the body. She considered cremation but soon came to the conclusion that every effort needed to be made to help her family accept his death. Touching a casket would help make it real.

Jeffrey had a lot of friends and family back in the town where he grew up. There was a family plot there he could be buried in, and the pastor that married them offered to preach the funeral. But Jeffrey and Sheila had lots of friends in Vermont too, and their pastor there offered to preach as well. She needed to decide who would sing and what songs to have sung. She had to figure out what to put in his obituary. And because Jeffrey had so many friends, she had to decide which of them would be the pallbearers.

On Sunday afternoon, hundreds of family and friends poured into the funeral home in Vermont. There was no time for her or the children to give way to their emotions and grief; nor was there time to buy a traditional black dress. Sheila really didn't care; she was struggling for survival. Their time was spent comforting others who were also suffering as a result of Jeffrey's death.

The funeral was on Monday morning; the church was packed to capacity. Then the family followed as Jeffrey's body was taken to his home church two hours away for a graveside service and burial.

The next two weeks were spent feverishly trying to take care of paperwork. Sheila's sister and brother-in-law stayed to help her make phone calls and set up a meeting with the Social Security Administration. Since Craig was a minor, he was entitled to Social Security benefits until his 18th birthday. Part of the life insurance could not be released until Jeffrey's will was probated, so Sheila immediately looked for the will. Jeffrey and Sheila had decided recently to make a few minor changes to the will, and she was sure they had put it in a logical place. However, it took two days for her to find it.

The funeral home was helpful by informing Sheila that she would need several copies of the death certificate. For months, any time changes were made that involved Jeffrey's signature, she needed one. After the will was probated, Letters of Testamentary were required to prove Sheila was the beneficiary of the estate. Because Craig was a minor, the court appointed an attorney to serve as Guardian ad Litem to represent his interests in the estate.

Even though she was Craig's mother, Sheila had no say as to who would be his attorney; nor was she allowed to be present when the attorney talked with Craig. This made her feel that her own son was a ward of the state. In the midst of Sheila's emotional upheaval and anger over the court's decision, she rested in the fact that she and Jeffrey had carefully planned by having a good will written by a reputable attorney. It cost Sheila $250 to probate the will and $75 for Craig's court appointed attorney.

Parenting young adults is not easy for two parents, but now Sheila had to guide them alone. Her oldest would soon return to his base in

Louisiana. He had gotten engaged to a beautiful Christian girl while he was home on leave; and, although Sheila was thrilled with his choice of a wife, she was very concerned about his taking on a family. Money management was not one of his strengths, and it had always been hard for Sheila to say no when he needed help.

She was glad her other two children were still at home. Her youngest son was still in high school. He was graduating with honors in a few months and had been awarded a scholarship to a reputable college. It depressed Sheila to think of him graduating without his dad there and moving away to go to school.

Brianne continued attending a nearby college to finish her education. She was dating a nice, Christian young man, and it looked serious. With so many changes taking place, Sheila didn't know how she could handle any more emotional stress; but, soon she would have to face that empty nest, and she no longer was looking forward to it.

While Spenser was home, Sheila's pastor had met with all of the children and challenged them to take as much of the burden off their mother as possible—to help relieve her stress. He also warned them that if they gave her any problems, they were going to be accountable to him. When they didn't carry their share of the load, Sheila pressured them. There were times during her emotional roller coaster rides she wanted to throw them all out of the house, even though they really hadn't done anything wrong. More than ever, she needed their support, and it was easy to try to make them compensate for Jeffrey's absence.

The company Sheila worked for was very supportive. For two months the employees divided into groups and provided meals once a week. The president of the company met with Sheila about her finances. He counseled her to put her money into short-term CDs and to wait a year before making any major decisions. His godly counsel paid off, because Sheila's first impulse had been to quit her job, sell her house, and move back to Virginia where her family was located.

After thinking things through, she decided to ride out the year. After all, she and Jeffrey loved Vermont, and this was where she had always wanted to settle down. Sheila had a good job and a wealth of friends who walked her through a valley of many tears in the following months. She relied heavily on their counsel and made herself accountable to her closest friends. Running away was not the answer to her grief. She had to work through it day after day.

No other church could have ministered to Sheila and her family in a more loving way than hers did during the first weeks after Jeffrey's death. It was apparent they had great compassion for her circumstances. However, they didn't understand the ongoing needs of widows and had no procedures established for helping to meet them. Although her pastor contacted her once in a while to see how she was doing, he had a hard time relating to her situation. He naturally stuck with the area he was most comfortable with—the spiritual. Unless people have been widowed personally or are trained, it is impossible for them to understand how to minister to a widow and her family.

Sheila was grateful for the support she did receive but, at times, she felt self-pity, especially when she felt lonely or things would go wrong at home and she didn't know what to do. No one seemed to understand what she had lost. She not only lost her best friend and lover, she lost her handyman, plumber, car mechanic, burden bearer, motivator, prayer partner, tax preparer, and source of inspiration. And he was gone forever.

Sheila's frustration with solving problems at home intensified as time went on. On one occasion, her toilets began to bubble and overflow, and her dishwasher wouldn't drain. Not wanting to deal with another problem, she reluctantly picked up the phone and called around to get the best prices to have it checked out. Thanks to Jeffrey's preparation, she could handle the expense, but she desperately wished someone else could have handled the problem or at least checked it out for her.

Apparently the septic tank had backed up and needed to be cleaned. The man who cleaned it informed her that down the road she would need to have new drain fields put in. She had never heard of drain fields. But sure enough, six weeks later the drain fields had to be replaced. Her backyard was a mass of wet mud.

So many people had told her, "Sheila, I can't even begin to imagine what you're going through. If there's anything we can do to help, please don't hesitate to call. We're just a phone call away." Where were they when she needed them? She believed they had good intentions, but help did not always come easily. Needs like a leaky roof or faulty wiring demanded immediate attention.

One time Sheila was in tears over an electrical socket that would not work. She began to panic when she thought about bad wiring and the possibility of a fire. Small problems seemed like mountains. She called a friend from the church for help.

"Ben," she said, "one of my electrical outlets has quit working. Do you know of a good, reasonable electrician I can call? I'm afraid it's the wiring, and I know how dangerous that can be."

Ben assured her that she didn't need an electrician. "Don't worry. I'll be over just as soon as I get a minute and we'll have it fixed in no time."

Sheila felt silly for getting so upset. But days later Ben had not come or called. She hated to mention it again, but he really had discouraged her from calling an electrician. She called again, and finally he came by one day shortly after Sheila got in from work. The whole time he was there, he told her how tired he was—he had really worked hard that day. Sheila realized right away that his heart was not in repairing the outlet. She really felt awkward about having asked for help.

After tightening a few wires and replacing the outlet cover, he said, "If this doesn't work, I'll come back and look at the wiring, but you may want to just use another outlet and leave this one alone."

Sure enough, it didn't work. Ben never returned and Sheila was frustrated again. She felt abandoned and vulnerable. She decided it was best to call someone she could pay to get repairs made when she needed them.

Another time, one of the men from her church told her that he would come and replace a few panes in the door that led from Sheila's bedroom to the balcony. It worried her that they were cracked and could be easily removed. After waiting at least a month, the man and his wife came by and he replaced one of the panes. He said he would return to install the other later.

When she finally got the nerve to call and ask about the other pane, the wife answered the phone and told Sheila, "Roger said you don't need to worry. No one is going to climb up two stories to get in your balcony door."

Sheila was hurt that the man was insensitive to her safety. One of the men Sheila worked with put her in touch with a good, reasonably priced handyman who had the job done within twenty-four hours.

Although some of her attempts to get help brought disappointment, others brought sacrificial responses. Two men came over one evening to repair the leak in her roof. One of the men (with permission from his wife) stayed five hours, working on the problem, even going after additional materials when he needed them. When Sheila encouraged him several times to go home and get some rest, he replied, "No, I'm not leaving until this is fixed." He didn't finish until after midnight, and he had to get up at by three o'clock in the morning to go to work.

A few Christian friends continue to help Sheila. Carol and James regularly take her garbage to the dump in their pickup. And James helps with lawn mower repairs and insists on mowing her lawn when Craig and Spenser are not in town. A car mechanic that goes to her church goes out of his way to help when she or Brianne have car problems. Other friends have helped by hanging doors, moving furniture, and replacing door locks.

* * * * * * * * * * * *

God's call to His church is to understand and minister to the ongoing needs of the widow. Churches should be trained in how to minister to the whole need, not just the spiritual need. Widows also have financial, practical, and emotional needs. Although Jeffrey and Sheila lived on a budget, she still needed guidance in managing her assets. A trained financial counselor that could meet regularly with a widow would help her become better prepared to manage her money.

Widows appreciate knowing that someone is praying for them on a regular basis. It gives them a feeling of warmth and security to know they're not forgotten. As much as a year after Jeffrey's death, Sheila saw different people who said, "Sheila, you are on my prayer list, and there's not a day that goes by that we don't pray for you."

But what good is it if you pray only? Practical needs are a great concern to the widow. All the chores, decision making, bill paying, and other daily problems at home now fall to her to handle. Most widows are very embarrassed if they have to call and ask for help. It would eliminate a lot of stress for the widow if the church should designate someone to call her and ask if she needs help with anything. Keeping a list of members and skills helps in delegating the project. If the widow doesn't have the money to cover the expense, her need should be presented to the benevolence committee for assistance.

Christians need to understand the fact that widows are hurting. The emotional adjustments in their lives are as significant as the physical adjustments that result from losing a limb. If the limb were a leg, a crutch or prosthesis would be needed to hold that person up.

God calls the church to be that kind of support for the widow. It's the tool He uses to help her balance as she gets up and tries to go on with the rest of her life. Often the wounds of grief slow her pace and she needs a reason to get up in the morning. She needs people to come by and visit her regularly, for at least a year, who will allow her the privilege of sharing her grief with them. Those who love deeply grieve deeply. This drains the bereaved of energy and concentration. Encourage the widow to build a relationship with the Lord. He stands ready to care for her.

Minister to her children. It touches the heart of God when people are willing to spend time with them. There is always a need for a godly father role model.

Although widows like Sheila learn to put their trust in the Lord as their source, God still works through people to meet needs. The challenge for the church is to be the vehicle God uses.

Many widows are faced with almost impossible circumstances because their husbands didn't plan properly and left them with virtually no assets. Often it is a misguided Christian who believes that having insurance is a lack of faith. If insurance is used properly—to provide—it is good stewardship. However, if you are over-insured, it can become a symbol of a lack of faith.

If a couple has been prudent and they are able to save enough to meet the family's needs in the event of the husband's death, then insurance may no longer be necessary. But for most families it is a means of providing in the early, critical years when funds are tight and a surplus is difficult to accumulate.

WORDS OF COUNSEL

If I could offer one piece of counsel to widows, it would be this: Let the other Christians around you know that you have needs—and be specific. Almost without exception the believers who know about a widow's needs will respond and help. The thing that keeps most widows from letting their needs be known is pride!

Your responsibility as a widow in need is to pare down your cost of living to where it is "reasonable." What is reasonable? This is often hard to define, but think of what you would expect of a widow you might be counseling who needed your support. You certainly don't need to live impoverished; nor do you need to trim all comforts out of your life. What is expected is a reasonable, balanced lifestyle. But then, that's really no different than God's plan for all of us.

I would suggest seeking a good financial counselor in your area to help you develop a budget. The budget should generally conform to the model found in Appendix A of this book. Every category must be funded or your budget won't work long-term. That means surplus funds for car replacement, clothes, insurance, vacations, and the like. These are all a part of our society, and there is nothing wrong with them if kept in balance.

If you're a widow, you may have found that your church readily responded during your initial crisis and was a great comfort to you at that time. However, if you're like most widows, you probably found that the church doesn't recognize that your needs are ongoing.

The void in a widow's life that her husband used to fill affects practically every area of her life. Usually he was not just the provider; he was her resident financial consultant, handyman, plumber, problem solver, car mechanic, or tax advisor.

Even if widows have adequate financial provision, they have to face the daily problems their husbands used to take care of and find other ways to fill the void. Suddenly handling all of the family decisions can make widows weary. Many of them need someone to consult with on crucial decisions.

During the grieving process, small problems can seem like mountains. They need someone who can understand and offer encouragement. They need someone knowledgeable enough to help evaluate problems and provide solutions. That alone relieves a lot of stress.

Widows who are parenting alone need friends who will help provide balance in their parenting and be mentors for their children. Those who are not adequately provided for may need their families to become more involved and to help with ongoing financial support.

In light of God's admonition to the church to care for them, widows often believe that their church should understand their needs. They become disappointed when people no longer respond readily or don't follow through with promises to help. It's embarrassing to have to ask for help, so they hesitate to plead their case. However, God holds a special place in His heart for widows and orphans, and their needs are important to Him.

Although widows have a responsibility to share their needs with others and allow them the opportunity to help, it's vital that they learn to put their trust and expectations in God alone to meet their needs. Then, if even the church doesn't respond to the needs, God can still help them through other people who are willing—Christian and non-Christian alike. He speaks to those who are willing to listen.

WILLS, TRUSTS, INSURANCE, SOCIAL SECURITY, AND TAXES

Information relating to these issues can be found in the Appendix. Also the companion workbook, *The Financial Guide for the Single Parent,* and the "What Every Widow Needs to Know" pamphlet cover these options in more detail. If you are interested in either one, call Christian Financial Concepts at 1-800-772-1976.

A PRINCIPLE TO REMEMBER
Widows need to establish a reasonable, balanced lifestyle.

"Gird your minds for action, keep sober in spirit, fix your hope completely on the grace to be brought to you at the revelation of Jesus Christ" (1 Peter 1:13).

Chapter 6

FACING THE JOB MARKET

The first time a single parent came into our offices for financial help I saw the reality of "too much month and too little money." She came at the encouragement of her pastor, whom I had met while teaching a seminar at his church. Nearly 20 percent of his congregation was made up of single parents, primarily divorcees.

They were attracted to his church because of a strong single parents' support group that was started by Sally, a church member who had been divorced in her mid-30s. Because she had experienced the trauma firsthand, she understood the plight of single parents. After her divorce she lost her home, car, and credit, and was faced with the prospect of raising three children on an inadequate salary and $300-a-month child support.

SALLY'S STORY

Before her divorce, Sally had been married ten years and had worked most of that time as a clerk with a national insurance company. Her salary was just about half of her husband's, which was okay while they were married, because her income allowed them to buy the things that a single income wouldn't have—a second car, two vacations a year. This all changed abruptly when the divorce was finalized. Her husband was directed to pay the credit card debts (nearly

$4,000) and to make the payments on her car for six months, in addition to $300 a month in child support.

Within six months he defaulted on the credit card bills, and Sally received notification that she was being sued for the debts. She contacted an attorney, who forwarded a copy of the divorce decree that assigned the debts to her husband. That stopped the lawsuit threats, but a few weeks later she received notice from the credit collection agency that her file had been turned over to a credit reporting agency. Her credit rating was lowered to the "bad debt risk" category, and from that point on she had no access to further credit and her card was canceled.

Her husband began to get later and later on his payments for child support. Then one month the check didn't come at all. She called his apartment only to find that he had moved—lock, stock, and barrel. Being in construction, his work location often varied and Sally was unable to locate him.

Month by month she fell deeper into debt, unable to pay her normal bills. One month she was juggling the electric bill, the next it was the gas, and so on. She lived in dread of the day the car would break down or one of the kids would get sick, because she knew she didn't have the money to pay for either. She thought about taking a second job, at night, but the cost of child care would have been nearly as much as she was making. Also she could already see the influence that the lack of supervision was having on her children. She feared that without some parental supervision they would begin to get into real trouble.

One month the inevitable happened: her car broke down. Fortunately it wasn't anything major—just a bad alternator. But the repair bill was nearly $100. The shop was insistent about being paid before she could have the car.

"Listen, lady, things are tough all over," the shop manager said caustically. "But my orders are absolute: Nobody gets their car without paying—in full. If you want your car, you'll have to pay."

"But I don't have that much," Sally pleaded. "Couldn't I just make payments for a couple of months? I'll pay them. I promise!"

"If you want to take out a loan, go to a bank. This is a car repair shop, not the Salvation Army," the manager said as he stuck her keys in his drawer.

In desperation Sally went to the manager of the office where she worked. "Mr. Lyle, I need an advance on my salary again," Sally said as she slumped into a chair.

"What's the problem now, Sally?" he asked sympathetically. He had several women just like Sally working in the office. He knew finances were a constant struggle for them and, to help them, he bent the rules whenever possible.

"My car wouldn't start this morning, so I took it into the shop near where I live. It's going to cost nearly $100 to get it out, and I just don't have the money right now."

"Sally, you always seem to be running behind. Isn't your husband paying you anything?"

"No, sir. The last check I received was over six months ago, and it bounced."

"Have you considered taking him back to court?"

"Yes, but no one even knows were he is. My attorney says it would be useless unless I want to swear out a warrant for his arrest. I don't even have the $50 it would take to do that."

"Sally, I really wish I could help, but the company has very strict policies against advancing money to employees. The branch manager sent me a memo just this week directing me to stop all salary advances. I'm sorry. But my church might be willing to help. We have a benevolence fund for needy people."

The words "needy people" struck Sally like a hammer. "But I'm not a beggar—or a street person. I don't need welfare," Sally said defensively. "I can take care of my own family."

"Sally, people helping people isn't welfare, and I don't mean to imply that you're a street person. But you need help, and others with a surplus are willing to help honest people in need. Any one of us could be in a similar situation."

"But why would your church help me?" Sally asked as she sat back down. "I'm not a churchgoer and I'm not especially interested in religion. I went to Sunday school a long time ago, but I didn't get much out of it."

"You don't have to attend church or be a Christian to qualify for help. Jesus said that we should care for the needy around us. I assure you, you won't have to join the church or even go to church unless you want to. But our rule is that we won't help anyone unless they talk to one of our volunteer counselors. All we want to know is that you're handling your finances as well as possible."

"Thanks, but I don't think so," Sally responded as she got up to leave. "We'll be okay. Something will work out."

"That's up to you, Sally. But, if you feel like you do need help, I'll be glad to call the church for you."

I certainly don't need anyone telling me how I should spend my money, Sally thought as she went back to her desk. *And we don't need welfare—from the church or otherwise.*

Out of desperation, Sally dipped into the utilities account she had set up to ensure that the lights and gas would always be paid. The company had sent her notice that the next time her account was overdue ten days or more they would turn her utilities off. *We have just enough to make it, she thought to herself . . . if we don't have any more problems. By the time I get paid again the utilities will be only nine days past due. I'll drop by the office and pay them in cash.*

A few days later Sally arrived at home to find another crisis waiting for her. "Mom, the mailman brought you a registered letter," her daughter yelled from her bedroom. "It's on the table."

An involuntary shudder went through her as she opened the letter. *What now?* she thought. *Doesn't it ever let up?* "Oh no!" she gasped as she read the letter.

"What's the matter, Mom?" her daughter asked, running out of her room at her mother's outcry.

"It's my car insurance. I completely forgot about it! Now it's been canceled. The state patrol says I've got to bring in my car tags and park the car until I can get insurance."

"How are we going to get around without a car?" Sandy asked in a typical teenager's manner. "Mom, we *need* a car!"

"I know we need the car, Sandy. You don't have to tell me that we need the car!" Sally snapped back. "And why don't you help clean this place? You and your brother make a mess and expect me to clean up after you. I'm sick and tired of being treated like a maid."

"Okay, Mom," she responded, obviously hurt. "You made your point, don't take it out on me."

Sally went about the task of preparing dinner, but inside she was in turmoil. *What am I going to do?* she asked herself. *I've got to have a car or I can't work. Even with the utility money I don't have enough to pay the insurance. And if I don't pay the utility bill they'll turn the lights and gas off. Then what would we do?*

The next day she went back to the manager's office. "Mr. Lyle, I need help," she said despondently. She went on to tell him about the insurance and the letter from the police. "What will I do?" she pleaded. "It's like I'm in a pit with no way out. Last night I even snapped at my daughter. If the pressure gets any worse I'm afraid I might crack up."

"Are you willing to talk with a counselor from our church to see if we can help?" he asked politely.

"I guess so. I don't have anywhere else to turn. I feel like I'm trapped."

"Sally, I don't want you to feel like you're being forced to do something you disagree with or that I'm trying to bribe you into seeing a counselor. I know from past experience that our counselors won't put any pressure on you as far as going to church is concerned."

"Okay, I guess I really don't have any alternatives. Would you call and make an appointment for me as soon as possible?"

"I'll do it right now," he said as he picked up the phone. He rang the church office and talked with the pastor's secretary. "Elizabeth, this is Bob Lyle. Could you tell me who is handling the benevolence ministry this week? Ralph Miller? Good, I'll call him now."

He then called the volunteer who was in charge of the benevolence program for the week. He explained a little of the situation and then put Sally on the line.

"Hi, Sally," Ralph Miller said cheerfully. "I understand you're having some temporary difficulties. We'd like to help, if you'll let us. Could you come by my office about noon? I'll have my wife meet us here and we'll take you out to lunch."

"Yes, of course," Sally replied, before she had a chance to think of anything else.

"Good, I'll see you here about 12 o'clock. Bob can give you directions."

At noon a nervous Sally drove up to the real estate office of Ralph Miller. "Oh, it's *that* Ralph Miller," Sally said out loud to herself. "I wonder why he would take time out of his schedule to see me? He's one of the biggest developers in the city."

Entering the large lobby Sally made her way to the receptionist's desk. "I'm here to see Mr. Miller, please," Sally said meekly.

"Yes, Mrs. Mulkey, he's expecting you. Have a seat and I'll tell him you're here."

A few minutes later Ralph Miller appeared. "Sally, welcome," he said. "Please come into my office. We decided to have some lunch brought in so it would give us a little more time to talk."

"Thank you, Mr. Miller. I know you're a very busy man, and I apologize for bothering you."

"Nonsense, Sally, and it's Ralph. You're the most important agenda we have right now. This is my wife, Rachel. Tell us a little about your problem."

Sally began to pour out her story, beginning with the problems she and her husband Paul had that ultimately led to a divorce. She went on to explain that Paul had stopped supporting them altogether and she had no idea where he was presently.

"Would you ever consider getting back together with your ex-husband?" Rachel Miller asked.

"No," Sally said emphatically. "My financial situation may be worse, but my life is a whole lot better since he's gone."

"I understand how you feel," Rachel replied. "I felt the same way about my first husband."

"You were divorced?" Sally said before she thought about it.

"Yes I was, Sally. But God, in His mercy, sent me a new husband. You see, my first husband was an alcoholic who would beat me up when he came in drunk. We had a beautiful home and lots of things, but our lives were a living hell."

"I know how you felt," Sally said honestly. "We didn't have a lot of things, except credit. But my husband drank too much and chased women. How did you meet Mr. Miller?"

"I met him after the Lord touched his life, Sally. You see, Ralph was my first husband too."

"You mean he's the same man who used to beat you up?" she asked in disbelief. "Yes I was, Sally," Ralph Miller said. "I'm not proud of it, but I believe I'm a new man now. And for the last ten years we've had a great marriage. Don't give up hope. God is still at work. I'm a walking testimony to that fact.

"Now, to deal with your problems. As I see it you have an immediate need to get your insurance paid and the utility bill caught up."

"Yes, sir. But I think I can take care of the utilities by the next paycheck," Sally said.

"Perhaps so, but that's going to put you constantly behind," Rachel added.

"It seems like I'm always behind," Sally replied. "I just can't make enough to get caught up before the next crisis hits."

"We see a lot of single parents who say the same thing, Sally. It's like an epidemic in our country today as the family continues to disintegrate through divorce and neglect. We would like to help you if you'll allow us to."

"I don't want any welfare," Sally said emphatically. "I just have a temporary problem and I'm willing to pay back any money that is loaned to me."

"Sally, I suspect you're not facing reality yet. Unless your husband is willing and able to help, you're probably facing a continuing problem—at least until your income improves. We're not in the lending business, and you don't need a loan. That would just cause you more grief when the notes came due. What I would like to do is take a look at your whole financial situation and go to the church with a proposal for how we can help."

"But I don't want my problems spread all over the church," Sally said defensively. "Maybe this just won't work out."

"Now Sally, you need to accept the fact that we're here to help," Rachel said. "The whole church won't know about your situation, only the benevolence committee, and I'll guarantee you that they won't mention this to anyone."

Sally, Ralph, and Rachel spent the better part of the next hour going over Sally's finances in detail. When they had finished, Ralph said, "I'm glad to see you have managed your funds well, Sally. Your problem is, you don't make enough income to meet all of your monthly expenses. I'm going to recommend to the committee that we pay your car insurance and supplement your income by $100 a month for at least the next year."

"You mean your church would do that for me? But I'm not even a member."

"You don't have to be a member of our church to need help, Sally. The Lord said that we are to help those in need. That was not limited to any particular group. By the way, we have an excellent single parents group at our church. If you ever feel like you just need someone to talk to who has been down the same road, I would encourage you to contact them."

"Oh, I'm not much for going to church," Sally said, looking down.

"You don't have to go to church, unless you want to. The parents' support group meets on Tuesday evenings at one of their homes. They usually have several people from outside the church who attend."

"I'll think about it," Sally said as she tried to accept what she had been hearing. "Can I ask you something?"

"Sure, go ahead," Ralph replied.

"Why are you and Rachel doing this? I mean, what do you get out of it?"

"Just the satisfaction of helping a fellow human being who is in need," said Ralph as he settled back into his chair. "You see, someone took the time to help me when I was down and out and I just want to repay the debt by helping others. Maybe one day you'll have the chance to help someone else too."

Maybe I will, Sally thought to herself. *I've been so wrapped up in my own problems that I forgot there are probably people out there with bigger problems than mine.*

True to his word, Ralph approached the benevolence committee with Sally's situation. Unknown to her, Ralph and Rachel committed to covering Sally's needs themselves and took on the responsibility to meet with her monthly to see how she was doing.

Over the next month Sally's financial situation improved. The additional funds helped meet some of the nagging budget items that she could never meet out of her own income. In addition, Ralph made it a point to see if he could track down her husband. He did so by contacting several friends in the building business. It turned out that he was working as a carpenter on a commercial project being built by one of Ralph's friends. One day after work Ralph and a member of the church deacon board knocked on the door of Paul Mulkey's trailer.

"Yeah, what do you want?" Paul asked rudely as he opened the door just a crack.

"My name is Ralph Miller, Paul. We would like to talk to you about your wife, Sally."

"Did she send you here?" he asked abruptly as he started to close the door. "You tell her if she doesn't want to live with me, I'm not paying her anything."

"Wait, Paul. Sally doesn't know we're here and she doesn't know where you live. You must realize you're in defiance of a court order to support your family. You don't want the police to show up here and arrest you, do you?"

Paul opened the door just a crack more so he could see the two men better. "You mean you haven't told the police where I am?"

"No, Paul," Ralph replied. "And we don't want to do that, if possible. Will you let us in so we can talk?"

Paul stepped back from the door and allowed the two men to come inside. The room was a total mess and furnished with only a threadbare sleeper sofa. "It's all I can afford," he said defensively. "I don't make much as a carpenter right now."

Ralph began the conversation by getting right to the heart of the matter. "Paul, I represent a local church that has been trying to help Sally meet her living expenses. We're not here to accuse you but just to find out who you are and why you're trying to avoid your responsibility to your family."

"Listen!" Paul shouted, "She left *me!* It's been just as hard for me as it has for her. She could come back anytime. But no, she said she would never come back. So let her do without for awhile too. Maybe she'll see it wasn't so bad before."

"Why do you think Sally left you, Paul?"

"Because she always wanted more than I could give her. She was always bringing up other people who had a lot more than we did. I did okay by her. After all, I'm not a college grad; I'm a construction worker. Sometimes I make a lot, and sometimes I don't."

"Paul, Sally said the primary reason she left was that you drank too much, especially when you were out of work."

"Well, maybe I did," he said, calming down a little. "But I felt like I was never good enough for her anyway. She may be smarter than me, but I'm still the man of the house."

For nearly two hours Ralph discussed the situation with Paul. Ralph then asked if he would be willing to meet with Sally and a counselor to try to work out their differences.

"I don't think she'll meet with me," Paul growled. "She might even have me arrested."

"Paul, if Sally wanted you arrested she would have already done so," Ralph told him. "After all, if we could find you, the police could too. Besides, you don't want to spend the rest of your life hiding from the police, do you?"

"No, and I do have most of the money I owe her. I put it in a savings account each week. I'm not a deadbeat like she thinks. I care about my children. I guess I just let my anger at Sally make me do something dumb. You tell her I'll start sending as much as I can each week and I'll send what I owe now by the end of the month."

"Why don't you call her and tell her yourself?" Ralph suggested.

"I can't do that. Every time we talk she gets down on me about something. I can't argue with her; she's smarter than I am."

A few days later a check for $800 came in the mail to Sally. As she opened the letter she knew that Ralph must have had something to do with it and she called him. "Mr. Miller, this is Sally. I just got a check from Paul, and he says he'll begin supporting us regularly. Did you make him do this?"

"No, Sally, I really didn't. We did go to see him, but he told me he'd been saving the money for you. It isn't that he didn't want to support his family. He was hurt over the divorce and was trying to get back at you."

The good part of Sally's story is that she and Paul were remarried about a year later. They still had many difficulties to work out, but the one factor they shared together was the acceptance of Jesus Christ as their Savior. Both were led to the Lord after attending counseling provided by the church. Sally's other story begins there.

She felt a conviction about helping other women in her circumstances, so she decided to begin a full-time support group for single parents. She accomplished two goals: (1) she made a commitment to be totally dependent on Paul's income, and (2) she was able to minister to others in need in her time of "plenty."

One of the immediate needs she recognized was the plight of new divorcees merging back into the work force. Many women who are divorced are either unemployed or underemployed. Many lack the basic job skills to provide for themselves and some are in situations that prohibit them from being reunited to their former spouses. Usually this is because of a remarriage, physical abuse, imprisonment, or the like. Obviously the goal of any Christ-oriented program should be to reunite families, but statistically the percentage of those who are reunited is less than 5 percent.

WHAT HAPPENED TO KIA

Kia came to my office as a result of being counseled by Sally. She was 20 years old, with a two-year-old son. She had gotten pregnant in her first year of college. Matt, a young man she had met only six months earlier, was the father. They moved into a small apartment near the college. Matt took a job delivering newspapers to pay their basic expenses. Kia had to drop out of college because of morning sickness. Matt struggled on for another semester, but the pressures of the coming birth and ever-increasing struggles of their relationship forced him to drop out too.

Once they were out of school and had left the friends they knew, their relationship continually declined. Even before the baby was born, Kia was spending as much time at her parents' house as she was with Matt, even though she had to deal with their disapproval. Unknown to Kia, Matt had developed a relationship with a young woman at the record store where he was working. Just before the baby was born he told her that he was in love with someone else and he was leaving. He immediately moved out.

For a short while she lived with her parents, but she and her mother argued constantly about the care of her baby and she decided to move out. Her dad paid the first month's rent on an apartment and the utilities deposits. She then began her search for a job to supplement the $150-a-month child support from Matt.

With few job skills and the need for at least $1,000 a month in income she received a rude shock: no offers. Ultimately she took a job in a retail store in the mall making $4.50 an hour, plus commissions. The job required her to work from 9 A.M. to 6 P.M., Tuesday through Saturday. Once again Kia was forced to ask her mother to keep her son.

Within two months it was obvious that she was not going to be able to make enough to hire a babysitter or put her child in a day care center. Even worse, she and her mother were again at odds over how to raise her son. One evening as she went to pick him up she heard her parents arguing. Her father was shouting at her mother that he didn't intend to raise another child, and it was time for Kia to take her kid home.

She stood outside the door for a long time just trying to shake the fear that rose up inside her. Inside she knew that what her father was saying was right. She had lived with Matt in spite of her parents' objections, and now she had to live with her decision. And he was probably also right that she didn't have a hope of being able to care for the two of them in the near future. She knew that she could not leave her son with her parents to raise when they resented her decisions.

That evening she collected their things and told her mother that she wouldn't be needing her for awhile and left. Unable to work, she had quit her job. She didn't even bother to go out looking for another one. She couldn't even leave her son while she was looking, and very few businesses would hire someone carrying a baby to the interview. *Besides,* she told herself, *I don't have the skills to get a better job anyway.*

She just laid around her apartment for another week until the money she had was gone. She was down to her last $3 when she called the county aid department and asked what she had to do to apply for welfare for herself and her son.

"Just come down tomorrow between 9 and 4," the woman said in a gruff tone of voice. "And be sure you bring evidence of your child's birth too."

"How much will I be able to get?" Kia asked meekly. By this time she was entirely intimidated by the woman.

"How should I know?" the woman snapped. "Listen, if you want help, come in. If you don't, then don't come in." With that she hung up on Kia.

She just sat there for several minutes as the tears formed. *How did I get myself into such a mess?* she asked herself. *It seems like there is no one I can turn to for help.* It was a sleepless night for Kia. She tossed and turned as her mind continued to go over her problems. But, having no other alternatives she could see, the next morning she got dressed and caught the bus downtown.

The welfare office was full of women with children, waiting to talk with one of the counselors. Kia sat down next to a large woman trying to manage three busy children. Seeing the anguished look on Kia's face she said, "This your first time here, Honey?"

Kia replied, "Yes, have you been here before?"

"Sure, Honey," the affable woman replied, restraining the now screaming children. "I tried makin' it on my own, but it just ain't no use. Every time I get a man he just ups and leaves. Welfare took my check away from me last time, so I'm just stayin' single." She looked at Kia and saw the tears in her eyes. "Listen, Honey, it ain't so bad. They'll give you $600 a month with one child. And if you can pick up some side money you'll be okay. I ain't gettin' rich, but at least we ain't goin' hungry no more."

Six hundred a month! Kia thought to herself. *That will hardly pay the rent and utilities.* "I can't get by on $600 a month!" she blurted out.

"Well then, child, you better move to someplace where you can, cause that's all you're gonna get here."

A depressed and defeated Kia spent the majority of that day sitting and waiting or talking to one social worker after another. "Have you tried to work?" one asked.

"Yes," was her reply, "but I couldn't make enough to live."

"Well, where was your last job? Did you make enough to qualify for unemployment? Do you have any family that will help? Do you have any savings? Are you pregnant now?" And on and on it went.

Finally, at the end of the day the last person she saw told her, "You'll be hearing from a social worker in the next couple of days to check on your living conditions. Do you have enough money for food?"

"Yes," she lied. By this time she was so frightened by the whole process she would have left willingly and forgotten the entire thing.

She was made to feel like a beggar, and her self-esteem was totally stripped away.

True to their word, the welfare system sent a social worker to interview Kia and then recommended that she receive temporary aid for dependent children. By this time she was down to virtually no food in the apartment and was nearly a month behind on rent and utilities. So even when the first check arrived it took nearly all of it just to get the urgent bills caught up. Kia knew she was developing slothful habits, including sleeping late and watching television nearly all day long. She rarely went out except to shop for food. Even then she felt like a second-class citizen when she paid for the food with food stamps.

It was during one of these infrequent outings that she saw a sign posted on one of the grocery store windows that read, "Out of luck? Feel like nobody cares? Call the single parents' support group, 555-5012." Kia thought about the notice all that day. She did feel like nobody cared whether she lived or died. Welfare helped her to survive, but only because she had a child to feed.

Every month she could feel her self-esteem dropping lower as the bills piled up. Now she had to dodge the apartment manager because she was over a month late on her rent. She had received two notices from the utility company, and Christmas was coming: a prospect that thoroughly depressed her. She and her mother were constantly bickering over her accepting welfare.

"Nobody in our family has ever been a beggar," her mother shouted over the phone. But she offered no help to Kia in paying her bills. Later that afternoon Kia dressed her baby and went back to the grocery store where she had seen the notice. She jotted down the number and went looking for a phone. When she rang the number she heard, "Single Parents' Support Group, how may we help you?"

It was the first time in a long time that Kia had heard anyone address her cordially and pleasantly. She answered, "I'm not really sure. I saw your notice in the store window and decided to call. What do you do?"

On the other end of the line Sally Mulkey quickly and efficiently outlined the support group she had helped to form at her church, ending with, "What is your name?"

Hesitantly, Kia answered, "I'm Kia Boatman. I didn't know you were a part of a church group. I'm sorry for bothering you. I'm not a churchgoer."

Quickly, Sally responded, "Please don't hang up, Kia. We're here to help you if we can. You don't have to be a part of any church." She went on to describe her circumstances when she had first asked for help. "Just having someone who cared whether I lived or died really meant a lot to me," Sally said. "I decided to see if I could help others as I had been helped. That's how our single parents' group got started. Could you come in, Kia? We really would like to help if we can."

"I'm sorry," Kia replied, "I don't have any transportation. I don't think I can."

"Well, I don't want to push you, Kia. But if you want to come I'll be glad to come over and pick you up."

"Why would you do that?" Kia asked, surprised by Sally's offer. "You don't even know me."

"Because you wouldn't have called unless you needed help. I want you to know that someone does care. Could I come by and pick you up?"

"No, that won't be necessary," Kia replied. She didn't know how to respond next. She was skeptical because of what she had heard about cult groups preying on desperate people.

After a couple moments of uncomfortable silence, Sally said, "I know you're wondering if we're some kind of weird group, Kia. All I can say is, you're welcome to call the church office and check us out. Also, if you feel pressured, just take your time and call me if you want to talk."

"No," Kia replied desperately, "I do need help. Could I come by this afternoon?"

Kia was but one of dozens of single mothers helped by Sally and her team of volunteers that first year. During the months of counseling the singles were separated into various categories of need. Almost all needed financial help, either temporary or long-term. Others needed immediate attention because of physical abuse or emotional problems. In reality, Kia was fortunate. She had no overwhelming debts; nor did she suffer from depression to the point of contemplating suicide.

85

She was first counseled by Sally to determine the extent of her problems, and then it was recommended that she meet with a financial counselor, just as Sally herself had when she asked for help. Since Kia's financial problems consisted primarily of past-due rent and utilities, the counselor recommended to the head of the benevolence committee that the bills be brought current—which they did from reserve funds. Then Kia was referred to another vocational counselor to evaluate her potential job options.

After giving Kia some aptitude tests, the counselor recommended that she be trained in word processing and data entry at one of the local technical schools.

"But how would I ever be able to pay for it?" Kia asked as the counselor outlined the recommendation. "And what would I do with the baby while I'm at school?"

"The committee has voted to pay for your training with a no-interest loan," the counselor said. "You can pay it back after you get a job that will meet your needs. Sally has arranged for some of the older women who have been helped by the single parents' group to baby-sit for you the three evenings that the classes meet."

"I don't know what to say," Kia said, almost crying. "You've done more to help me than anyone in my life."

"That's why the Lord put us here," the counselor responded. "Maybe someday you'll be able to help someone else, just as Sally is doing with you."

The counselor then went on to ask Kia about her spiritual life, knowing that she had grown up in a local church—but quite obviously without a personal relationship with Jesus Christ. As is often the case, he had the privilege of leading Kia to the Lord, building on the foundation laid by Sally and her volunteers.

Kia completed the training course at the technical school and was eventually hired by a Christian businessman from the church. At first the finances were extremely tight and she required help from the benevolence fund on several occasions: to pay her car insurance premiums, to buy a small car from one of the other members, and to cover some medical expenses. After a year she was offered a job as a court recorder and trained by the county government. Within another year she was making nearly $30,000 a year!

Unfortunately, Matt married someone else, thereby removing any hope of reconciliation. Two years later Kia married an attorney she met through her job. Both are Christians, serving in their own capacities. He is one of the church's referral advisors, and Kia is a financial counselor and teaches a single parents' financial workshop in the church.

HOW TO FACE THE JOB MARKET

One of the many needs of single parents is to have jobs with adequate incomes and health benefits. Through the development of the Career Pathways department at Christian Financial Concepts, it was discovered that most people with low incomes are unhappy with their jobs, and most people who are unhappy at their jobs are not suited to their jobs. The greatest guarantee of job promotion and satisfaction is matching the right person with the right job. Most people don't realize they have been designed for a unique purpose. Career choices are often based on money, prestige, peer or parental pressures, or just taking jobs to get paychecks.

Career Pathways offers several tools for assessing personality, interests, work values, and skills. The complete career assessment addresses all of these areas through a comprehensive, twenty-five-plus-page report generated for each individual. It includes a step-by-step action plan, a career planing guide, and a job sampler that lists career groups of more than 800 jobs. For most effective career guidance at the lowest price, the complete assessment should be utilized. However, the complete assessment may be out of the price range for many single parents; therefore, it would be a good idea for churches to provide this service for them, based on what they can afford to pay.

Two other resources that the individual can use to gain insight into career direction are *The PathFinder* (by Lee Ellis) and *Finding the Career That Fits You* (by Larry Burkett and Lee Ellis). Both books are available at Christian Financial Concepts or your local Christian bookstore (see below for phone number and Internet information). The first is designed to assist those who already have a good understanding about their interests. It provides practical steps for choosing the right career field, searching for a job, and writing a résumé—plus it gives pointers on how to successfully interview for a job.

The latter is a self-assessing workbook that examines a person's interests, skills, and work priorities. The self-assessment may be difficult for some individuals to analyze properly; they may need to work with someone to complete it. The workbook also includes information on drafting résumés and contact letters, job search strategies, managing finances, and self-employment.

Other resources being developed through Career Pathways are a curriculum for training career counselors in the local church and special software for generating assessments. For information on Career Pathways materials, call the materials department of CFC at 1-800-722-1976 or visit the Internet site (http://www.cfcministry.org).

Job skills can be recognized and developed in a variety of ways. One single mother volunteered for her church and made some great discoveries about her talents. Linda was working at a job she hated, but she felt she had no choice since her education was limited. She had always had creative desires but ended up working with computers all day doing data entry.

To fulfill her desires she started volunteering in the drama department of the church. She organized and assisted so well that soon she was appointed assistant drama director. An opportunity for creative writing came when the music director had music for a drama presentation but could not find the right script. Linda volunteered to edit one the church had used before. She took the project home and completed the script in a short period of time.

Linda was a little anxious about how the first performance would go, but when the choir performed it, the church was thrilled. Her talent was confirmed and she was asked to write more. She was given access to a church computer and was asked to do the newsletter for singles. Eventually, she was hired as a secretary at the church and was responsible for the Sunday bulletin, the church newsletter, and any other creative writing. She decided to take writing classes at a local junior college and eventually landed a job at a Christian advertisement and publishing company in creative writing.

The church can do so much to assist single parents in developing their skills and talents by providing personality assessments, computer training, creative outlets, classes in how to write résumés, and job contacts. Many single parents have been knocked down emotionally and need encouragement. They need to know they are needed and that they can offer something valuable, especially if they are receiving benevolent assistance.

A PRINCIPLE TO REMEMBER
God often provides beyond the need level.

"If you then, being evil, know how to give good gifts to your children, how much more shall your Father who is in heaven give what is good to those who ask Him!" (Matthew 7:11).

Chapter 7

FACING THE ISSUES

It would be great if all the situations facing single parents worked out as well as that of Sally, whom we met in the last chapter. Many times we like to think that when someone, such as Sally, commits her life to the Lord, He will miraculously intercede on her behalf and cure the problems. Unfortunately, it doesn't always work out that way. God doesn't force His will on us, and unless both spouses are willing to listen and to obey God's direction, one of them may walk away from the marriage.

All too frequently a wayward spouse will even rationalize his or her actions on the basis of instruction from some misguided counselor—Christians included. In such circumstances it is difficult to do much more than comfort the grieving party as much as possible. Unless and until the spouse recognizes the error of his or her way, no amount of counseling will help.

It often sounds like a cliché to say to someone whose mate has left and cannot be persuaded to return, "Pray about it and turn him (or her) over to the Lord." But in reality, that is the exact prescription given in God's Word according to Philippians 4:6, *"Be anxious for nothing, but in everything by prayer and supplication with thanksgiving let your requests be made known to God."*

In most no-fault divorce situations, both parties are actively seeking to get out of the marriage. In the heat of constant arguments and financial pressures, divorce looks like a viable, even attractive, option. However, what frequently happens is that the problems get worse for both parties after they separate. We have looked at a few examples of women and men whose marriages dissolved and their financial situations got worse; but that is the norm, not the exception.

Sometimes the opposite is true. When the marriage dissolves, the wife is able to generate a greater level of income and her situation appears to improve. We all probably have met one or two divorced people who remarried the "perfect" man or woman and lived happily ever after.

Unfortunately, the church wants to believe this situation is the norm. It is not. Family, friends, and even church leadership frequently encourage single parents to start dating, perpetuating the belief that one can just start over and forget the past, even when there are children involved.

Even unwed mothers naively believe that keeping the child will somehow enforce the connection they had to the father and they will marry. Unfortunately, this usually is not the case. The commitment, family connections, and identity that should have been established through marriage are not established, making it much easier for someone to just walk away. Marrying someone other than the child's natural parent presents another set of problems. It's a rare stepparent that can truly accept someone else's child as his or her own.

There are some fundamental principles that deal with the subject of marriage and divorce. In spite of what our "enlightened society" says, these have not changed. If I could accomplish one thing through this book, it would be to convince any married couple that they are better off married than divorced, if they're willing to work at it, regardless of what they feel or have heard to the contrary.

GOD ORDAINED MARRIAGE

From the beginning, God designed marriage to be the ideal setting for perpetuating the human race. He developed the union to consist of a man and a woman, committed to each other for life and to raising their offspring. God knew that a mother and a father were needed to create the best environment for children. As they state their marriage vows, couples are warned not to take this union lightly. Violating this union with premarital sex or adultery or unbiblical divorce has dire consequences.

Statistically, figures indicate that the healthiest children are raised in their original two-parent families. Statistics further indicate that the greatest guarantee of poverty in the U.S. is to be raised in a single mother's home. In addition, children from single-parent homes are at higher risk of experiencing emotional problems: hyperactivity and withdrawal; educational problems, such as lack of attentiveness; and difficulty delaying gratification. They tend to hang in peer groups that are more apt to have behavior problems: smoking, drinking, or early and frequent sexual experience. In more extreme cases, they are more likely to commit drug abuse, suicide, vandalism, violence, and criminal acts.[1]

In fact, daughters from single-parent homes are twice as likely to become teen mothers,[2] and 70 percent of young men in prison grew up without fathers.[3]

THE SUBJECT OF DIVORCE

In our generation divorce claims 50 percent of all first marriages. Although the number of never married single parents attending church is still small compared to societal demographics at large, it is estimated that 40 percent of all church members have been divorced at least once. In light of this, one would logically think church leaders —pastors, deacons, elders, and the like—would make marriage commitment and divorce the topics of most of their teaching. Instead the church has skillfully skirted the issues, lest they offend too many of the "flock."

It would be difficult to assemble a board of deacons or elders in most churches if the biblical admonition against a divorced person serving in these capacities were applied absolutely. Obviously the same could be said of other qualifications, such as the management of their children, the love of money, their reputation outside the church, and so on. But for the purposes of this section, we'll limit the discussion to divorce.

How many sermons have you heard taught on the subject of divorce as a sin? Not many, I suspect, unless your pastor is an individual without fear of reprisal. It could be argued that to attack the topic of divorce is to open wounds in the lives of many people. That is true. Not many divorced people would counsel others to get divorced. Those who have lived through the hurt and rejection of a divorce know what they are talking about. More often than not it's the unrepentant person who deliberately chose to abandon his or her commitment who is offended. In fact, they look to the church to approve and condone their actions many times. "After all," they say, "who could live like a Christian in that situation?"

Someone sent me a set of cassette tapes from a large fundamental church where one of the church leaders had taught a series called, "The Five Reasons Why Divorce Is Biblical." It was clear that this teacher himself was divorced and remarried. He was totally convinced in his own mind that God had told him to divorce his first wife because she was a hindrance to his "ministry." In his thinking, his new wife was obviously God's perfect mate for him.

Later I heard that this church had several staff members who had gotten divorced while serving there. They obviously felt the calling of God to find their perfect mate also. Students in the church's Christian school were being exposed to the same material, and I rather suspect they will use it as justification to shop around until they find the perfect spouse. This teacher eventually became involved with several female students and was removed from his position—but not until a lot of damage had been done to impressionable young people.

Contrary to what any teacher today tells you, God says, *"Everyone who divorces his wife and marries another commits adultery; and he who marries one who is divorced from a husband commits adultery"* (Luke 16:18). I find it difficult to read anything else into that passage. That doesn't mean divorce is the unpardonable sin, any more than other acts of disobedience; but to even hint that divorce is an acceptable cure for marital problems is akin to blasphemy.

I understand the arguments used in conjunction with verses like Matthew 5:32: *"But I say to you that everyone who divorces his wife, except for the cause of unchastity, makes her commit adultery; and whoever marries a divorced woman commits adultery."* But in Matthew 19:6 the Lord tells us *"Consequently they are no longer two, but one flesh. What therefore God has joined together, let no man separate."*

Take it on the counsel of God's Word: If divorce is allowed for any reason, it is only for immorality. And even so, there is no indication that divorce must be the alternative. It would depend on whether the offending party repents and asks for forgiveness.

A PRINCIPLE TO REMEMBER
Vows are sacred promises not to be broken.

"A poor, yet wise lad is better than an old and foolish king who no longer knows how to receive instruction" (Ecclesiastes 4:13).

YOU CAN MAKE IT WORK

There are times in nearly every marriage when it seems barely tolerable. I know that was true in my marriage for the first several years. Judy and I came out of non-Christian backgrounds, with little or no training in a good marriage relationship. Consequently we argued about nearly everything. My days were filled with work and school; hers were filled with children. We found our free time to be incompatible. I wanted to study and then do nothing; she wanted to get out of the house and go somewhere. These situations made for some big arguments and hurt feelings on both sides.

We live in a generation that has not been taught the importance of keeping vows. Today it is socially acceptable to file for bankruptcy with no concern for repaying the creditors who extended trust in the form of money. Certainly some people are forced into bankruptcy, but the vast majority choose it as a legal means to avoid an unpleasant situation. Often the lessons aren't learned and the symptoms reoccur time and time again.

Contract law is so detailed that the average couple has no concept of what they are signing. The most successful lawyers are those who can word agreements so their clients can escape without penalty, if necessary. Often the basic intent is not to ensure that both sides are fairly represented but, rather, to provide a means of escape if circumstances change.

Unfortunately, the same also can be said of marriage. The words

95

"until death do us part" don't really have any significance to many couples. Marriage is entered into with the idea, "if it doesn't work out, I can always get out." With that basic assumption in mind, a marriage seldom will work out. There are just too many potential areas of conflict between two virtually independent people.

It is only when two people make an absolute commitment to each other that a marriage can function as God intended. It is unrealistic to think that conflicts won't occur. They will. But if spouses know that both of them are irrevocably committed to the marriage, the problems can be resolved. However, if one spouse is always walking on eggshells for fear of his or her partner bailing out in a conflict, the stress will create even more conflict, and the situation will escalate beyond control.

AGAIN...AND AGAIN...AND AGAIN

Perhaps my most unusual marriage counseling situation was with a couple who had been divorced and remarried (to each other) three times.

Jack and Marcia were married while he was a pilot in the Air Force. As is normal for military personnel, Jack was shipped around the world periodically, and Marcia was left to oversee the packing of their things and then follow along later. She was a registered nurse and had been totally self-supporting for several years prior to their marriage. The frequent moves put a tremendous strain on their relationship, especially because Marcia could no longer work as a nurse, except as a fill-in.

They made an adequate amount of money, but it was always tight financially. Since Marcia actually had more free money before they were married, it placed an even further strain on their marriage. Their first child was born shortly before Jack was due to be released from the service. What neither of them knew was that this child would be born with several abnormalities that would necessitate multiple operations.

Jack already had accepted a position with a major airline as a flight engineer. Contrary to popular opinion, new flight engineers aren't paid extremely well; and, with the loss of base housing and free medical care, they actually netted less than they had made in the service.

The health problems with their child again necessitated that Marcia not work, except on a part-time basis. Since the airline's insurance excluded the preexisting medical condition of their child, they ended up with several thousands of dollars in medical bills.

They struggled through the first year in civilian life, barely making it financially, and their communications level declined steadily. Then Jack was offered a chance to move up to copilot with another airline at a substantial increase in pay. Marcia naturally thought the increase would resolve their financial situation and allow her more money to buy things like furniture, clothes, and a new car to replace her 10-year-old one.

What she hadn't counted on was how cheap Jack was when it came to spending money on creature comforts. He was a very security-conscious person who always thought in terms of long-range goals, the first of which was to save for their children's college education. When Marcia pointed out that they didn't have children, just one child, Jack reminded her that such thinking was typical of a woman's mentality.

As you can imagine, from that point, communication between them went downhill. Despite Jack's vehement objections, Marcia accepted a full-time nursing position at a local hospital. She worked the third shift, and during the times when Jack was traveling she hired a live-in babysitter.

The real battles began when Jack attempted to impose restrictions on how Marcia could spend her money. His priority was additional savings; hers was the purchase of creature comforts. After a particularly bitter argument one evening, and while Jack was gone on a trip, Marcia opened her own checking account and applied for her own credit cards. She effectively separated her finances from those of her husband.

When Jack discovered what she had done, he was furious. We'll pick up the conversation there.

"Marcia, if you want to find yourself living alone, you're definitely on the right track," Jack said bitterly.

"Well, maybe I do," she responded just as bitterly. "You know, Jack, you're about as cheap a human being as ever walked the face of this earth. I'm tired of living like we don't have two pennies to rub together. If you won't buy the furniture we need, I will!"

"Oh no you won't!" Jack threatened. "I'll throw it into the street. I'm the head of this family, and I decide what we buy or don't buy."

"You've got a lot to learn about what being a husband and father is all about," Marcia shouted in his face. "When you discover what it is, you call me. In the meantime Becky and I are moving out."

"Go ahead, see if you can make it on your own. You'll come begging for my help before a month is out."

"I wouldn't ask you for anything if our lives depended on it," she screamed. "I'd be afraid we might divert some of your precious money."

That evening Marcia moved into a motel room and, a few days later, into an apartment near the hospital. The first few months were a struggle, but then she was made shift supervisor at a substantial increase in pay, and things got easier. She loved Jack but knew they had irreconcilable differences. *We're so opposite, we'll never be able to get along,* she thought.

The next month Marcia filed for divorce. When Jack was served with the papers he was totally shocked. He knew, as she did, that they were having serious problems, but he never considered the reality of a divorce. To him it was just an idle threat he had used in the midst of anger.

After several attempts to dissuade Marcia from the divorce, Jack realized it was hopeless. In the meantime Marcia found out she was pregnant with their second child. She decided to say nothing to Jack and went through with the divorce. It soon became obvious that she was pregnant, and Jack seemed to develop a totally different attitude toward her. He would bring her small gifts, which was totally out of character for him. From time to time he even would buy a nice piece of antique furniture and give it to her. They saw more and more of each other and finally Jack proposed that they get remarried.

Marcia was hesitant at first because she had more freedom on her own, as well as more spendable income, but gradually Jack won her over and she agreed.

They were remarried in a small, private ceremony and returned to their previous home. For a while things were different. Jack really tried to ask Marcia's counsel on what she felt they needed. He would even ask her opinion about a potential investment he was considering.

Marcia began keeping the checking account but, lacking Jack's bent for detail, she made several critical mistakes, including allowing the checkbook to go unbalanced for three months. Then one day Jack was bringing in the mail and noticed a letter from their bank marked, "Urgent information—respond immediately." When he opened the letter, he found a delinquent balance notice and overdraft charges amounting to $60. He blew his stack.

"Marcia, what is this?" he shouted at her without warning.

"What is what, Jack?"

"These overdraft charges. Don't you keep the checkbook balanced?"

"I let it go a couple of months because I got busy with the new baby, but I knew we had enough money in our account."

"Well it's pretty obvious we didn't." Jack fumed. "That's it, Marcia, I'm taking over the account again. You just don't have any common sense when it comes to money."

She started to put up an argument but realized it was useless. Jack was back to his old habit of worrying about money all the time. She realized she should have been balancing the account and apologized, promising Jack she would do better.

"Oh no you won't!" Jack shouted as he threw down the paper he was reading. "I'll keep the checkbook from now on. You haven't got the brains to manage money."

Jack's caustic comments cut Marcia to the quick. In spite of her education and success as a nurse, she had always suffered from an inferiority complex. From that point, their relationship continually deteriorated, until a few months later Marcia decided to leave again. The one thing that made her life totally intolerable, she said, was that Jack didn't trust her to handle their money.

"It's like he is penny wise and pound foolish," Marcia said to her best friend, Laura, one afternoon, a week before she decided to leave. "He resents it if I want to buy a couch or a chair, but then he'll go out and invest $10,000 in some new deal. I feel like I'm a slave in my own home."

"You don't need to put up with that," Laura told her. "I'd leave him if it were me. You can make it on your own. You're not a child; don't let any man treat you like one."

The more Marcia thought about what Laura said, the madder she got. *He is treating me like a child,* she thought. *I don't need this.*

Two weeks later she and her daughters moved out. Six months later she and Jack were divorced again. This time Jack decided that he'd had enough also and determined that he wouldn't even try to see Marcia again.

But as is often the case, the Lord had other ideas. Jack became ill with a stomach problem that required him to be hospitalized. While in the hospital he contracted a staph infection that became life threatening. Marcia heard about it through a mutual friend and came to visit him. Being a nurse she recognized the seriousness of his illness and ultimately stayed on to care for him when he left the hospital. It probably was her concern and care that saved Jack's life.

It took nearly a year for Jack to be restored to full health and flying status. During that period Marcia provided the majority of the income by working weekends at the hospital. Finances were extremely tight, but Marcia proved her capabilities by managing all the finances and making ends meet. Often it required shopping at thrift stores and buying dented cans and day-old bread, but they made it.

Jack asked Marcia to remarry him near the end of that first year. She was reluctant to do so even though she realized that she loved him. "Jack, you have never allowed me to share your life before. You and I are different people, but somehow you've always acted like I should fit into your idea of the perfect wife, which seems to me to be a non-person. Do you really think you can share your life with me and allow me to be myself?"

Jack's response was, "I've learned a lot about needing other people, especially you, over this last year. I know I can. Will you marry me?"

Marcia said yes and they were remarried, again in a very quiet ceremony.

As Jack got back on his feet and resumed his career, many of the old habits returned. When they had virtually no money he was willing to accept Marcia's help, but now that he was making in excess of $100,000 a year again he took over the finances. Once more their lives became one argument after the other—always over money. Within two years of their second remarriage Jack left and filed for divorce.

This time it was Marcia who was convinced the marriage was over for good. She was emotionally drained of all feelings, or so it seemed to her at the time. Several times she said she seriously considered suicide. The only thing she felt had stopped her was her daughters' need for her. The firstborn had become a timid, frightened child as a result of all the upheaval in her life. Marcia even had to withdraw her from school for a period of time because she would get hysterical when left there.

Fortunately Jack was supporting them adequately this time, so work was an option for Marcia, not a necessity. She had relocated several states away from Jack, trying to get her own life back together.

Jack began to drink periodically—and then often. He was well on his way to becoming a "down time" alcoholic when, by chance, he was flying with a copilot, Andy Greer, who recognized that Jack had some real problems. Andy made it a point to maintain contact with Jack and often asked him to attend a meeting of the Fellowship of Christian Airline Personnel. This is an organization made up exclusively of airlines employees who meet monthly to share Christ.

Jack's usual response was, "I appreciate the offer, Andy, but religion just isn't for me. I don't have any need for a crutch."

"I can see that, Jack," Andy said with some intended sarcasm. "That's why you drink when you're not flying though, isn't it? You need to get away from reality."

Jack's emotions flared. "What I do is none of your business or anyone else's. I do my job, and I'm good at it."

"I agree," Andy nodded. "You're an excellent pilot. And if that's all there was to life, you'd do great. But life goes on after flying, Jack, and one day we'll both be faced with the fact we can't fly anymore. Then what?"

For the next several weeks Andy continued to ask Jack to attend one of the meetings with him. He could see Jack's life slipping into a Jekyll-and-Hyde pattern—the efficient pilot and the drunken civilian. Finally Jack agreed to attend a meeting, simply to get Andy off his back.

At this particular meeting, an ex-Air Force fighter pilot gave his testimony about how Christ had come into his life while a prisoner of war in Vietnam. He also shared how he and his wife had never been able to get along before because of their differences over money.

The more he talked, the more Jack saw his own life, altered only by the different circumstances. He went away from that meeting a changed man—not from the outside yet but from the inside. He willingly attended several more of the meetings; and each time he felt the speaker was talking directly to him. By the fifth month Jack had become a regular attender, had begun to actually read the Bible, and was asking Andy questions about Christianity every time he saw him. Finally Andy asked him, "Jack, would you like to have Jesus Christ as your Savior?"

Jack thought for several moments without responding. He had always known that something was missing in his life. No matter how much money he made, he was always fearful of the future. The more he tried to be a good husband, the more he fouled up his and Marcia's lives. His drinking was becoming a daily problem now, and even when he flew he found himself needing another drink. Suddenly he realized that it was God who had been calling him all these years. He just hadn't recognized the voice. "Yes I would, Andy," Jack said as he began to pour out his heart. "My life's a mess and I ruin everything I touch."

That day Andy led Jack to the Lord. Jack's conversion was one of those Damascus road experiences. He never had the desire to drink after that day. He joined a good church that Andy recommended and, most importantly, began a consistent walk with the Lord.

He tried several times to call and talk to Marcia, but she refused to speak with him. Then one evening, after an all-day trip, he decided to go see her. The next morning he was knocking on her door.

Marcia opened the door to see a red-eyed, rumpled pilot, still in his uniform standing in her doorway. She naturally assumed he was drinking and in some kind of trouble.

"What do you want?" she said curtly. "Jack, if you need help, go somewhere else, would you?"

"I don't need help, Marcia," he replied as he saw himself in the window next to the door. "I know I must look crummy but I haven't been drinking. In fact, I don't drink anymore. I just need to talk to you for a few minutes. After that I'll go, if you want." Jack spent the next two hours sharing with Marcia what had happened in his life.

Clearly skeptical, she said, "Are you sure this isn't just another one of your side ventures, Jack? I thought things had changed last time, but we're so different and you want someone you can rule over. That won't be me."

"I know you have a perfect right to feel that way. All I ask is that you give me a chance to at least see you and the girls for awhile. I feel so totally different inside now. I believe I am a different person."

Something in what Marcia saw told her that Jack was different, and she agreed to see him once a month on Sundays. This relationship continued for nearly a year, with their feelings for each other gradually being restored. In December of that year, Jack asked Marcia to marry him once again. She agreed. Only this time they were remarried with a full ceremony. Jack decided that since he was a new man, this would be a new marriage.

Over the next year together Marcia did indeed see a new man in Jack. He still had some bad habits, but the difference was that he had a humble spirit and readily admitted his faults when he blew it. In a move totally out of character for him, he asked Marcia if she would be upset if he voluntarily took a demotion from pilot to copilot.

"Why in the world would you want to do that, Jack?" she asked. "Wouldn't that mean a cut in pay too?"

"Yes it would," he replied. "But I would really like to get more involved in winning others to Christ, and as a senior copilot I can choose my own schedule more than I can as a captain."

This so totally floored Marcia that she didn't really know what to say. She had seen changes in Jack over the year they had been remarried but never one so totally out of character. She replied, "Whatever you want, that's what I want too, Jack." Marcia began to cry as Jack put his arms around her.

That day Jack had the privilege of leading his wife to the Lord, just as Andy had done for him earlier. These events occurred nearly seventeen years ago. Jack and Marcia are still married. They now have three children and Jack is an internationally known speaker for Christ. Marcia heads the local Right-to-Life Counsel in their community and writes for several Christian magazines on the emotional and psychological problems of abortion. Both she and Jack agree, the fourth time's a charm.

MARRIAGE DECISIONS

With the burdens of finances and raising kids alone, some single parents become desperate for the wholeness and help provided in a two-parent family. Unfortunately, finding someone becomes a priority. Many times single parents will even compromise their values to find someone to rescue them.

If you're a single parent, thinking about remarriage, consider the fact that over 70 percent of second marriages end in divorce, and about 85 percent of third marriages end in divorce. I know this is not what single parents want to hear, but it needs to be said. Christian single parents seem to think they are immune from the statistics, but they're not.

If you spend any time at all with single adults, you'll realize there are plenty of Christians who have gone through the breakup of a blended family. And those who remain married will tell you how difficult it is to keep the family together. I have seen, as you may have, the occasional blended family that is secure and well balanced, but they are more rare than we would like to believe.

The problems associated with raising children in a blended family are often greater than the problems of single parents. As previously stated, second marriages have a much greater risk of failing than first marriages. Therefore, many Christian psychologists believe it is better for most single parents to remain single until the kids are grown, especially if the children have already reached puberty.

Children in the highly charged teen years are difficult for most intact families, but parents in blended families also have to contend with their children's already developed family roles, jealousy, past hurts, and feelings of intrusion from "outsiders" into their pre-existing family. In fact, for the best chance at success, some counselors recommend that the oldest child should not be over five to six years of age when a second marriage occurs.

The Bible gives clear instructions regarding remarriage. These guidelines should be considered diligently before making any decisions. Of course, the most appropriate remarriage would be to your former spouse.

The exception seems to be young widows. Paul mentioned in

1 Timothy 5 that younger widows should *"get married, bear children, keep house, and give the enemy no occasion for reproach."* This would be good advice for the never married parent as well, especially if he or she marries the child's other parent. Many times that is not possible. After the never married parent comes to repentance and right relationship with God, they too should consider marriage. Solomon said in Ecclesiastes 4:9-10: *"Two are better than one because they have a good return for their labor. For if either of them falls, the one will lift up his companion. But woe to the one who falls when there is not another to lift him up."*

God designed us to live in pairs, but His ideal is that we marry one spouse for life. You have to determine for yourself whether it is God's will for you to be married. And, unless you're widowed, you need to determine whether you believe you have biblical grounds to marry. Then, if you meet someone special, you need to determine if this is the person God brought into your life for marriage. Finally, if you believe you're ready for marriage, you need to look at some of the more common problems you may face.

PRENUPTIAL AGREEMENTS

Agreements between two people contemplating marriage are becoming more common in a society that plans for divorce before the marriage begins. Unfortunately, many of these people are Christians who have been deceived by the world around them into believing that they must protect their assets against a future spouse. To do this merely allows Satan a foothold in the marriage that he will exercise at his leisure.

There are some circumstances in which a prenuptial agreement may be biblical, as well as logical, and we will examine these. But, for the most part, they drive a wedge into a relationship that will quickly turn into a rift, under the right set of conditions.

MY STUFF, YOUR STUFF

One example I recall vividly was that of Jan and Mike. Jan had lost her husband three years earlier through an automobile accident. Mike had lost his wife two years earlier after a long struggle with diabetes.

Jan had received a settlement of nearly $500,000 from the death of her husband. This, along with $200,000 in life insurance proceeds, provided her a comfortable living. Mike, on the other hand, had been a missionary when his wife was diagnosed with diabetes and had returned to the United States to seek treatment. During the intervening five years, he had worked as interim pastor for several churches, just barely scraping by and accumulating some sizable medical bills.

Mike and Jan met at a church missions conference where he was a guest speaker. His message was on the time he had spent in the jungles of Central America. Jan was so impressed by his humility and gentle spirit that she asked him home for dinner one evening.

Their relationship developed over the next several months, with neither of them discussing their financial situations. It was obvious, though, that Jan lived comfortably and Mike lived very frugally. They freely discussed their previous spouses and how difficult the transition to single life again had been. Within a year Mike had proposed to Jan and she accepted.

When she told her children about the impending marriage, they hit the ceiling. We'll pick up the discussion at this point as Jan talks with her oldest daughter, Megan.

"Mother, you hardly know this man," she said sharply. "How do you know he's not just out after your money?"

"Mike's not like that, Honey. He has never mentioned money to me."

"Sure, but he can see you're pretty well off," Megan said caustically. "That money was provided by Daddy and I don't think it's right that some stranger should get it if something happens to you. You need a prenuptial agreement, so if the marriage doesn't last or you die the money will belong to us kids."

"I don't know if that's a good idea. Mike might think I don't trust him," Jan said as she thought about how such an agreement might affect Mike.

"So what? If he's really not after your money, he won't mind. If he does, you'll know he's a phony."

After several similar conversations with her other children, Jan decided she should talk it over with Mike.

"Mike, my children think we should have an agreement about the money that came from my husband's death. They feel it should go to them if something happened to me," Jan said sheepishly as they sat in her living room.

"I agree totally," Mike said. "That money belongs to your family. I wouldn't want it, no matter what. God has always provided for me and He will continue to."

"Then you are sure you won't resent it if we have a prenuptial agreement?"

"Absolutely not, Jan. I wouldn't want to do anything that might jeopardize your relationship with your family."

Jan had the agreement drawn by her son-in-law, who was a practicing attorney. It was very explicit that whatever assets were brought into the marriage by either party would be passed to the heirs upon the death of that person. The document went on to require an accounting of all assets and liabilities just prior to the marriage by an independent accounting firm.

Mike signed the agreement even though, within himself, he knew that the very concept of a prenuptial agreement was wrong. If the circumstances had been reversed, his decision would have been absolute: he would never have held his assets away from Jan. But because he was basically broke and Jan had the assets, he felt that to say anything would be viewed as covetousness on his part.

Jan had the same basic feelings about the agreement but hesitated to voice her feelings because of the pressure from the children. This was amplified even further when they saw the accounting of their estates. It was clear that Mike owned virtually nothing and, in fact, owed nearly $40,000 from previous medical bills.

Based on this new information, the children began to put pressure on their mother to further stipulate that none of her assets could be used to pay Mike's bills. She struggled with this new restriction, but finally caved in to their insistent pressure.

After Jan shared once more with Mike how her children felt, he said, "Jan, no relationship can be built on anything other than mutual trust and dependence on God's Word. I don't seek or desire anything you have, but I also cannot be anything less than the head of my own household and still be worthy of teaching others. I believe it would be best if we call off our wedding. I wouldn't want your children, or you, to ever feel I had taken advantage of your material wealth. But I would rather remain single than feel that we are less than one."

"But Mike, I love you," Jan said as she realized that he was serious about dissolving their relationship. She began to realize what Mike said was right; her children were reacting from totally selfish motives.

"I love you too, Jan," Mike said honestly. "But I love the Lord first and foremost, and I believe God has given me this test to determine if I would compromise what I know to be right just to keep peace in your family. Remember what our Lord said, *Any kingdom divided against itself is laid waste; and a house divided against itself falls*" (Luke 11:17).

For the next several weeks Jan did not hear from Mike, though when she saw him in church he was pleasant and courteous. As time passed she realized that he would not change his mind. She spent many fitful nights wondering if she had missed the Lord's direction in her life.

Several months later she learned that a Christian businessman in their church had paid all of Mike's medical bills so that he could return to the mission field. He was gone nearly three years before she saw him again. She was absolutely determined to ask his forgiveness for her doubting attitude and had written several times, inquiring about him. Each time he had responded with a polite, but "arm's length" answer.

When at last he returned from the mission field, Jan was devastated to learn that he had recently been married to a missionary's widow he had met in Central America. She had learned a lesson about conforming to this world's image, rather than to God's, and she had learned the hard way.

In Genesis 2:24 we see the example of the only perfect marriage between a man and a woman in all the Bible. It is Adam and Eve before sin came into their lives. It is ordained, *"For this cause a man shall leave his father and his mother, and shall cleave to his wife; and they shall become one flesh."* The Lord confirmed this relationship: *"Consequently they are no longer two, but one flesh. What therefore God has joined together, let no man separate"* (Matthew 19:6).

God desires that a husband and wife be one working unit, literally one person. How can two be one when they divide their assets into two parts from the beginning? The material things are not the problem. They are merely the outside indicator of inside problems. As the Lord said, *"He who is faithful in a very little thing is faithful also in much; and he who is unrighteous in a very little thing is unrighteous also in much"* (Luke 16:10).

I have counseled several couples who had prenuptial agreements. As best I know, none of them were benefitted by the agreement and most were divided by it. More commonly, it is a woman bringing assets into a second marriage who seeks a prenuptial agreement. Usually this is the result of a bitter experience from a first marriage—or else from bad counsel from those around her.

Obviously, we see many prenuptial agreements in the secular world as celebrities trade marriage partners as easily as most people trade automobiles. These relationships rarely last more than a few months, or years at best, and often still end up in bitter court battles. They must never be the pattern for Christian relationships.

WHEN IS A PRENUPTIAL AGREEMENT ACCEPTABLE?

When an older couple get married and neither has need for the finances of the other, an agreement can be made that all the assets will be held in trust for the lifetime of either surviving spouse. If the funds are not needed, the trust will be distributed to the heirs of the first spouse upon the death of the second. This effectively gives a couple total access to the funds if needed. But if they are not needed, the heirs are guaranteed the residual assets.

In this example there is no violation of the biblical principle of oneness. The assets would be available but are held in reserve unless needed. I have seen this type of prenuptial agreement used quite effectively many times. Often it is not what the heirs might want for themselves, but it does assure the financial support of the surviving spouse without diverting one spouse's assets to the other's offspring.

HIS KIDS, MY KIDS, OUR KIDS?

When two people who both have younger children get married, the situation can get very complicated when it comes to asset distribution. Often this is a source of potential conflict within families. A widow or widower may bring considerable assets into the marriage that were provided by the first spouse's family. The family often wants to maintain some control over the assets, even though they were given without reservation initially.

Jody was a widow with two children. Her husband Ken had died in a boating accident. Ken's family had provided the funds for their home and a sizable trust fund for their family. The trust in Ken's name was payable to his widow (Jody), and the trusts for their two children were under her control, though stipulated for the education and support of his children only.

Jody had been a widow for nearly three years when she met John, a widower with two children, through their church single parents' group. After dating for several months they decided to get married. Ken's mother was extremely agitated with Jody's decision. John was a teacher and had virtually no assets other than a salary. Ken's mother, Pearl, didn't appreciate the idea that John would be benefitting from Ken's trust.

"I want you to guarantee me that the income from Ken's trust won't be used to support that man!" Pearl said pointedly, as they sat having lunch at her club.

"I can't do that, Mother Hayes," Jody said politely. "John will be my husband and the father to Ken's children too. I can't keep my finances separate from his."

"He's not the father of my son's children," Pearl protested, as she threw her napkin down on her plate. She was not used to people contradicting her.

"I know he's not their birth father. Ken was. But Ken is gone now, and I want to get on with my life. John's a good and honest man who will love all of our children."

"He's a leech who knows a good deal when he sees it," Pearl said callously. "I'd like to see him support two families on his income."

"But, Mother Hayes, the Lord has made it possible for us to combine families. I know it is through your generosity to Ken and your grandchildren but, after all, it all belongs to the Lord."

"I still don't want my money used to support some deadbeat," Pearl almost shouted. She always got angry when Jody tried to spiritualize everything that happened. *Even when Ken drowned, she didn't hurt like I did,* Pearl thought to herself.

"Mother Hayes, I will be glad to assign the trust back to you, as I have offered before."

"No, you can't do that! Then you'll have my grandchildren living in poverty too. I won't have that." Besides, Pearl knew that her husband, Ken Sr., would not allow the trust to be returned.

He had often said, "Pearl, you need to let go and allow Jody to live her own life. You can't use our money to manipulate her and the kids."

"Then you will have to allow me to decide how the funds will be used," Jody replied respectfully. "When John is my husband, we will share all things in common. Ken would have wanted it that way too."

Sure, because he was brainwashed by that church they went to, Pearl thought. *Ever since he got religion, I lost him as a son. He could have run his father's business one day and married a girl his equal. Instead, he became a campus minister and married someone whose father was a truck driver.*

After Jody and John were married, Pearl continued her attacks, only now directed at John. She never failed to remind him that he was living on her money and was little more than a leech as far as she was concerned. Whenever she would have the grandchildren over for a visit, they would become belligerent for weeks after returning home. Often they would echo their grandmother's sentiments.

When John would give them directions, they would reply, "You're not our father. We don't have to do what you say. Grandmother Hayes told us so."

Finally, in exasperation, Jody and John confronted Pearl. "Mrs. Hayes, John said as they stood in her library, "I know that you don't approve of Jody's remarriage. But she and I are one and we're trying to do the best by all the children. Jody is going to have another child and we want all the children to accept each other as equals."

Pearl interrupted, "Ken's children will have the best that money can buy. They can afford to go to the best schools."

"That's true," John agreed, "but for right now they're just children who need the love and discipline of their parents. Jody and I have decided that we will no longer use any of the funds from Ken's trust. Also we will not allow the children to draw any funds from their trust, except for college, which is a long way off."

"I won't have it!" Pearl said bitterly. "I will not have my grandchildren living like paupers. You don't make enough money to provide for your family."

"Perhaps not by your standards, Mrs. Hayes. But Jody and I have worked out a budget that will allow us to make it. And I have begun to sell some articles to some magazines. We will make it!"

"Well, I won't allow it!" Pearl shouted as her husband, Ken Sr., came into the room.

"Won't allow what?" Ken Hayes asked.

"They seem to think they can get by on his salary," Pearl said, fuming. "And they said they won't allow the grandchildren to use their trust money either."

"Good for you!" Ken said to John and Jody. "A little suffering will do those kids good. Pearl seems to forget that we didn't inherit our money; I earned it. And we had some tough times early on. I believe it helped to build the character I saw in Ken Jr. as a young man. He never was impressed with money, and he did what he believed was the right thing to do."

The next four or five years were times of financial struggle for John and Jody, as well as all their children. But as John's income improved, through his writing, they were able to buy a home. Throughout their grammar school and high school days, the boys all slept in one bedroom, the girls in another.

They grew close as a family, and John's persistent loving attitude won over Ken's children. As they grew into teenagers they read some of their father's notes on his ministry work and realized how little he counted material success as important.

This was one family that overcame the troubles of "his and her" kids, but it was only because their strength was firmly rooted in the Lord. Without that, and without Jody's total commitment to honoring her husband, their path might have been significantly different; as were those of other couples I have counseled.

GOING IN BLIND

Jeff and Karen were married for twelve years when they divorced.

Jeff always believed that they had a satisfying, stable family life. He was shocked when Karen told him that she was interested in someone else and no longer in love with Jeff. When she moved out, she took their daughter Jenny with her. However, she soon found out that her new boyfriend didn't want Jenny around, so she gave full custody to Jeff.

Jeff's job as a mechanic provided enough for the two of them, but he felt a great void in his life, and was sad for Jenny since she didn't see her mother very often. He began attending a nearby church to expose Jenny to some good female role models. He became a Christian a short time later and quickly became actively involved in the church.

With a new relationship with Christ, new Christian friends, and lots of church activities, his void began to diminish. In a short time, Jeff believed once more that he and Jenny had a stable, satisfying family life. He didn't date much. He found it difficult to trust women in dating relationships. It was easier if he just remained friends with them. The last thing he was looking for was a new wife.

Janet was an independent, talented, competent woman with a bubbly personality. She was an executive at a nearby bank, and she was well respected by everyone. Even though she was divorced, she served in many leadership capacities at her church. Her former husband drank and had run off with another woman over ten years before. She had become very content with her single status and had lots of close friends.

Shortly after her divorce, Janet had given her heart to the Lord, and because she was so happy in her new relationship with God, she never took time to really heal from the wounds of her divorce. Consequently, she always had a secret fear of close dating relationships.

Jeff and Janet met at a singles conference in a nearby town, and they were immediately attracted to each other. They both decided to start seeing each other as friends and had a great friendship for almost a year. Jeff's romantic feelings were growing and he couldn't ignore them. He shared his desire for a dating relationship with Janet, but she resisted at first. She loved Jeff, but she didn't want to make another mistake. She said she needed more time.

She prayed, searched the Bible, and talked to everyone about it. A couple of the things concerned her. She felt she was more spiritually mature than Jeff, she had been a Christian longer, and she made more money than Jeff. Most everyone she talked to agreed that these issues could result in some serious problems in the future.

Janet agreed to start dating Jeff, but she wouldn't set a wedding date right away. Waiting would help to ensure that this was the right thing. After another year, Jeff began to pressure Janet for a commitment again. She had gotten comfortable in their dating relationship and agreed to set a date for the following year. She could still come and go as she pleased and could stay involved with all the ministries she wanted. She also could spend her money as she pleased.

Six months before the wedding, Janet and Jeff began premarital counseling with their pastor. The pastor was already aware of the potential problems and began dealing with them right away. Let's pick up the conversation there.

"Janet, what does it mean to you when you think about Jeff becoming the head of your home?" Pastor Stan asked.

"Oh, I think it's going to be wonderful not to have to make all the decisions anymore. I believe I'm ready to share my life with someone again."

"You've been a Christian longer than Jeff. Do you think that will be a problem?"

"Oh no," Janet responded. "Jeff is growing in the Lord. There may be some areas in which I may have more experience, but we usually talk about them. I think, with a strong wife, Jeff will grow very rapidly."

"What about income? You make more money than Jeff, and sometimes you have to travel in your job. Do you see any problems with that?" the pastor asked.

"Well, I'm sure there are going to be some adjustments to be made. We're going to live in my house since Jeff doesn't own one. He'll have to change jobs because his job is too far away. Jeff knows I'm generous with my money and that I travel. He doesn't think it's going to be a problem, so neither do I. Besides, I probably won't be traveling as much after another year. So, I don't think it will be much different than the way it's been for the last two and a half years. I think we have a realistic view of the situation," Janet replied.

Pastor Stan changed his focus. "Jeff, let me ask you the same questions. What does it mean to you to be the head of the house?"

"I believe the man is supposed to be the head of the house. He needs to listen to his wife and consider her opinion, but the final decision is his. I've been raising my daughter alone for five years, and I was married before that. I know how to be the head of the house. And I think Janet wants that because she's handled so much on her own. Of course, I would trust her spiritual wisdom on things; she's a very spiritual person," Jeff answered confidently.

"What about the money and travel and changing jobs?" the pastor continued.

"Janet is an independent woman; there's no doubt about that. She's done a lot for herself—come a long way. But she's a very loving woman. I believe she would make sacrifices if it were necessary. Jenny and I have lived alone for five years, so I don't think Janet's occasional trips will mean that much and, like she said, it's not going to last that much longer. We can discuss when she needs to be generous and when she needs to back off. And besides, Jenny really loves her. So do I," he said affectionately towards Janet, who was smiling at him.

"You mentioned Janet's spiritual maturity. Is that a threat to you?"

"No. Oh no. I realize she's been a Christian longer. She knows more Scripture; she understands some things more. That's okay. I'm not intimidated. I can hold my own when I need to. As long as she respects me as the head of the family, it won't be a problem."

Jeff was sure he understood Janet, and Janet was sure she understood Jeff. The pastor brought up the problems several more times in counseling. The two insisted they could handle the problems. After all, they weren't children anymore.

As could be expected, Jeff and Janet were married, and the problems began to come. At first it was little things, like Janet's involvement in church activities. Jeff expected she would want to spend more time as a family with him and Jenny.

Then it was her lack of preparation for things. When she was ready to take a trip, she packed the morning of her flight and usually was running late and had to run for the airplane. Jeff couldn't understand why Janet had to have hats, shoes, purses, and jewelry for every outfit. She had a lot of outfits and he didn't think it was all necessary.

Plus, she continued to give money to every cause that came along. Jeff was making less money in his new job and had a hard time dealing with Janet and their budget. He believed in giving—but not half of their income. She had a family now; she needed to think about things, to plan for the future.

And they needed a house—one that was theirs, not just hers. And she needed to quit spoiling Jenny. *She's a good kid, but she won't stay that way if she gets everything she wants.*

Janet was getting irritated that the house had to be cleaned constantly and that she was expected to cook meals. Jeff did a lot, but she wasn't used to it. She could take them out to eat, but Jeff wanted meals at home. She was tired from working so much, and she was discovering that children don't seem to pick up after themselves as much as they should.

Jeff's tightness with money was starting to annoy her. They had enough money; he just didn't have enough faith. Besides, she needed to look nice for her job.

Janet also wished Jeff would just get more involved at church; then he wouldn't care if she spent so much time there. She was needed, and he should realize that. And he needed to let her be more of a real mother to Jenny. She was a woman and had instincts he didn't have. Janet was just loving Jenny, who had been through so much and didn't have a mommy to love her.

Jenny was the least of Janet's problems, just as Janet had imagined. Jenny very rarely spent time with her real mother and Janet thoroughly enjoyed being the "mom." She doted on Jenny and bought her new clothes and new toys. She got upset when Jeff was being too firm with her. She would often give Jeff a "woman's perspective" when she felt that she could handle the situation better. But if Jeff insisted he was right, she usually agreed. After all, Jeff reminded her often, she had never raised children.

The problems escalated all through the first year. Jeff and Janet shared some of their problems with some of their friends. They even went back and talked to Pastor Stan. By that time, Jeff and Janet disagreed on just about everything. Pastor Stan reminded them of their commitment to work the problems out. They had discussed these issues before, and they said that they could handle them. He pleaded with them to try harder. The first years are always the hardest.

Janet knew it would work out if they just gave it time. After all, spiritual maturity is a growth process. Jeff would get it and she would be more understanding. The first thing Jeff asked her to do was stop spending so much money on clothes and accessories. Janet said she could do that. She started shopping at sales and thrift stores.

She was really proud of how she was handling the money. She even waited for special occasions to buy something fun for Jenny. And she relaxed a little more on the house looking perfect. But when Jeff asked her to cut back on her traveling and time at church, she balked. This was her job and she couldn't change that. In fact, they were in a crisis at work right now and she probably would be working more evenings and weekends when she was in town. She agreed to spend a little less time at church if Jeff would get more involved.

Jeff was beginning to feel like he'd never gotten married. Not only did he feel like he was still handling everything alone, he also began to feel "kept": He was living in her house, living mostly off her money. And he didn't like to feel spiritually inferior to Janet. Every time they argued, she would explain her situation spiritually and then back down to keep peace in the family. Jeff became more involved at church, but Janet didn't slow down.

Eventually, she came to church one Sunday morning in tears. She told us Jeff had left and taken Jenny with him. She said that he was really upset and that their marriage was over. He couldn't take it anymore. Jeff moved his things out and filed for a divorce soon after that. He said he'd made a terrible mistake marrying Janet. Janet, on the other hand, believed she had done everything she could to save her marriage. She was bewildered and devastated. She not only lost a husband again; this time she lost a daughter too.

* * * * * * * * * * * *

I don't know why we can't look at things realistically before things get out of hand; but, generally, people enter into marriage with their eyes closed. I've heard it said that you should keep your eyes wide

117

open when choosing a mate, then close them tight after marriage. When kept in balance, that's pretty good advice.

PLAN FOR A FUTURE WITH HOPE

Many single parents carry around loads of pain, usually in the form of guilt, fear, shame, and anger. Most of those who were abandoned through a divorce or separation have usually tried everything they could to reconcile their marriages, yet their spouses still left, or married someone else, or just refused to reconcile. They often feel like miserable failures. Even those who feel their divorce or separation was justified deal with these emotions.

Never-married single parents suffer too—from guilt and shame when they realize they've acted contrary to God's Word and the best interest of their families. And although widows did nothing to cause their single parent situation, the usual pain most grieving individuals experience may be intensified by fears and doubts about the future. Trusting God in areas that used to be handled by a spouse is often difficult and frightening.

No matter how you became a single parent, I assure you, your sin or situation is not too great for God. He offers forgiveness and healing for you and your children when you come to Him with a repentant heart. He cares for you and about your situation. The Bible tells us that He has good plans for those who come to Him—plans with a future and a hope.

If you're still carrying around a load of pain, why not take a few minutes right now and take that burden to Him. Healing and growth in the Lord is a process. You may have to take your burdens to Him daily or even hourly if your wounds are new.

If you've never trusted God with your life, remember, His Word says He stands at the door of your heart and knocks. You must open the door. And when you open your heart to Him and ask Him to forgive you, He will, because He is faithful and just.

Not only does God forgive, but He removes your sins as far as the east is from the west. That's never-ending, because the east and west can never meet. He even forgets they ever existed, because He loves you and chooses not to remember. He is such a gracious Father. You and your children couldn't have a better one for your family.

A PRINCIPLE TO REMEMBER
Though every person fails, God is faithful.

"Trust in the Lord with all your heart, and do not lean on your own understanding. In all your ways acknowledge Him, and He will make your paths straight" (Proverbs 3:5-6).

1. *The Index of Leading Cultural Indicators,* William J. Bennett, Heritage Foundation, 1993.
2. "Better Family Values," *Christianity Today,* 1995.
3. "World News Tonight with Peter Jennings," American Agenda, *Growing Up Without Fathers,* 12/13/94.

Chapter 8

HOUSING, CARS, AND KIDS

The three big expenses in any single parent's budget are housing, cars, and kids—in that order. As the kids get older, the order shifts to put them first. But in the early years most single parents struggle to find adequate housing they can afford. A little later in this book I offer some budget advice that will help most single parents. But for right now we need to address these three budget busters.

HOUSING

The average American family (making approximately $32,000 a year) will spend about 35 to 40 percent of their net income (after taxes and giving) on housing. This amount, about $750 per month, seems inadequate in many parts of the country. But when compared to the $350 to $400 that most single parents have to spend, it seems like an impossible dream.

Most single parents know the frustration of looking for an apartment, much less a home, for which the total monthly expenses (rent, utilities, telephone, and so on) must be $400 or less. Ultimately many single parents migrate to run-down neighborhoods where the crime rate is high but the rents are low.

Brittany was one such parent. She was recently divorced after four years of marriage and had one child. Her ex-husband, Tony, was a drug user and dealer who had been arrested and sent to prison shortly after their divorce. Brittany worked as a typist in the local county's tax office with an annual salary of $13,000.

She had become a Christian through a ministry that evangelized door to door. She regularly attended a small independent church, where she was well supported spiritually. But since many of the other members were also single parents, many with greater needs than hers, she realized that she could not expect much financial help from the church. In fact, Brittany herself often gave to the needs of some of the other single parents in the group.

While married, their finances had cycled from almost nothing to thousands a month, as Tony bought and sold drugs. When she guessed what he was doing and confronted him, he denied it, claiming that the money came from winning bets at work. Finally, when she realized he was on drugs himself, she knew he must be dealing them and begged him to get help. Tony categorically denied any involvement in drugs, even when she found several stashes of drugs around their apartment.

People began coming to their door late at night, and Tony would sell them drugs and take the money. Twice he was accosted at gunpoint, and even she and the baby had been threatened by a drug addict. Finally she left and relocated in a small apartment. She felt fortunate to secure the job with the county, since it also provided health insurance.

Shortly after she filed for divorce, Tony was arrested and, within six months, was convicted, sentenced, and shipped off to prison. Brittany quickly found that her income would only cover the bare necessities, and the $475-a-month rent was beyond her meager salary. She went shopping for an apartment within her budget and was quickly discouraged. The only thing close was a run-down apartment in the center of the known drug district. She refused to locate in this area and realized that something had to happen or she would eventually be forced out of where she was.

She discussed her problems with her single parents' support group that met Wednesday evenings in different homes. We join them there.

"You know, I'd be willing to work more, if I could," Brittany said to the group of six women and a man who met that evening. "But by the time I hired a babysitter I'd be lucky just to break even. Besides, who would I find to keep my little girl in the evenings?"

"I don't believe God wants you to abandon your daughter," one of the other women said. "You wouldn't see her except on weekends."

"I know it," Brittany said as the tears came. "It's already hard enough. Last week my little girl started calling her babysitter 'Mommy.' It almost broke my heart. The first words she said were to a stranger, instead of her mother."

"You can always go on welfare," one of the women said. "At least that way you can stay home with your kid."

"Yeah, how much does that pay though?" another woman said in a disgusted tone. "Maybe $600 a month. So you get to stay home with your kids and beat the rats off too. No thanks, I want somethin' more out of life than bein' a government ward. I've lived in those welfare houses before. I'll work three jobs before I'll do that again."

The discussion lasted for the better part of thirty minutes before another woman, Maye, spoke up. "You know, we're totally ignoring the basic principle—that God provides for our needs. Maybe that's why He has us here tonight. We all share similar problems. Right?"

"Right!" answered everyone.

"Brittany, I'm having the same kinds of problems you are. My money just won't stretch far enough to cover all my living expenses, and my ex-husband pays his child support every month. But if we pooled our resources together, we'd have enough money to meet both our needs."

"How could we do that?" Brittany asked.

"By renting an apartment large enough for both of our families and sharing expenses. I'd like to go to school in the evenings and learn about computers, but I can't afford a babysitter either. If you could watch my daughter a couple of nights, I'd be glad to do the same for you, if you need it."

"Hey, that's not a half bad idea," one of the other women said enthusiastically. "What about that, Brit?"

"I'll have to give it some thought," Brittany said as she considered the idea. "What if we don't get along though?"

"If we can't make it work as Christians, then we have a fundamental problem with God's Word, I'd say," Maye replied. "Besides, what do we have to lose? Do you have a better idea?"

Brittany had to admit that she didn't have any other viable ideas. By the next week she had decided to give it a try, and within another week she had located a three-bedroom apartment that was only slightly more than her present apartment. The next month she and Maye moved in.

The first few weeks were a real adjustment for the two families as they went through the normal territorial disputes of who got the shower when, and who cleaned up the dishes when. But within a month they had worked out a plan that assigned jobs to each in turn, and things were progressing relatively smoothly.

All the expenses were split down the middle and they even found that they could share rides, except on Maye's school nights. By merging the two incomes they had effectively created a family situation with slightly more than an average income available. All the bills were paid and each was able to begin building a small savings.

Brittany found one of the available solutions to housing costs for single parents: to combine their buying power and pool resources. Unfortunately, too often our independent spirits as Americans keep us from doing that. We don't want the bother of merging our lives with someone else's because of the inconvenience.

A look at some of the immigrants, coming from other countries to the U.S., is an enlightening experience. They usually will combine two or more families' incomes in one home to conserve expenses. Each family makes the sacrifices necessary to achieve their long-range goals: to own their own businesses, eventually.

As Solomon said in Ecclesiastes 4:9-10, *"Two are better than one because they have a good return for their labor. For if either of them falls, the one will lift up his companion. But woe to the one who falls when there is not another to lift him up."*

There are other housing options available to the single parent who is willing and able to work and will use some ingenuity. I wish I could take credit for many of the ideas I have shared with single parents over the years but, in all honesty, most of them I've learned from single parents who had found solutions to their dilemmas.

Eileen was a 40-year-old mother of three children who ranged in ages from 6 to 18. Her husband, a deacon in their church, had run off with his 30-year-old secretary (and mother of four herself). When he left, he also cleaned out their savings account, leaving Eileen with $300 dollars to her name.

Fortunately several members of her church rallied around her to help pay the bills that were coming due. Her job as an administrative assistant to a school superintendent would provide only about half of the current expenses in their home.

Shortly after her husband left, Eileen received a call from the mortgage company, informing her that the house payments were two months in arrears, and if they were not paid immediately the lender would begin foreclosure proceedings. A friend from her church checked on the mortgage for her and discovered that Eileen's husband had taken out second and third mortgages to put money into his failing business, forging her name both times.

Suddenly, within a month she was faced with expenses that were double her income, a home going into foreclosure, and mortgages that totaled more than the value of the home. Needless to say, she was in a state of shock.

On the advice of an attorney from her church, she contacted the mortgage company vice president, told him the details of her situation, and offered to sign a voluntary foreclosure to save them the legal costs of evicting her family. The loan officer was sympathetic but could do nothing to delay the legal action prescribed by his company. He did, however, arrange for Eileen to stay in the home for another month by paying rent equivalent to the total monthly mortgages. Since this sum was the equivalent of her total income, she knew something else would have to be worked out.

As she began the search for a place to live, it became obvious that even an apartment sufficient for a family of four would be too expensive on her salary. She was willing to rent a two-bedroom apartment or home, but most landlords wouldn't agree to do so. Finally she found one who would, and she rented a two-bedroom apartment for $500 a month. This took almost 50 percent of her take-home pay. After tithing to her church and paying the note on her car, it left her slightly more than $300 a month for everything else. Her 18-year-old daughter, Jamie, worked afternoons and weekends while attending the local junior college but could barely pay for her clothes, food, and transportation out of her part-time income in a fast-food restaurant.

Eileen realized that her friends from church wouldn't be able to support her deficit for any long period of time. As with most Americans, Christians included, most lived on what they made and it was their normal giving to the church that had been diverted to Eileen's need.

Jamie came to her one evening and said, "Mom, I can't let you carry this burden alone. I'm going to drop out of school and get a full-time job so I can help."

"What would you do, Honey?" Eileen said as she hugged her daughter. "Work in a hamburger place? No, you stay in school. God has an answer; He always does. We just don't know what it is yet."

"But Mom, I don't mind, really. I can always go back later, when things get better."

"If the Lord wants you to be a chemist, you have to go to college. If you drop out you may never have the chance to go back. No, we'll wait awhile and at least give God a chance to show us His way."

"Why do you think God let Daddy do what he did to us, Mom?" her daughter asked as they hugged each other.

"I don't believe God had any part in what your father did. He made his own choices and turned his back on the Lord. He will have to account for it one day. If not in this life, then in the next. We can't let something we can't change make us bitter. Then the enemy would have two victories."

Eileen struggled on for another two months, barely staying even with the help of friends. Then one evening when she went to pay her next month's rent, something happened that would alter her circumstances significantly.

Instead of finding the resident manager of the complex in his office, there was a new face. Eileen asked, "Where is Mr. Newton?"

"He doesn't work here anymore," replied the pleasant woman in a business suit. "I had to let him go."

"Oh," Eileen replied, not wanting to appear too nosey. "Well, I came to pay my rent. Can I pay you?"

"Yes," the woman answered. "I manage this complex as well as twelve others."

"Thirteen apartment complexes! That must keep you busy. How do you have time to collect rents?"

"I don't. But it's really hard to keep apartment managers. Mr. Newton was a nice enough man, but he didn't keep good records and apparently didn't maintain the complex very well, according to the complaints I have received."

"I've only been in my apartment for three months, so I don't really know. I do know I tried to get someone to fix our leaky faucets, but nobody has come yet."

"Several tenants have had similar complaints. This month alone we had three families move out because their apartments had problems that hadn't been handled for months. If you know of someone looking for a job as an apartment manager, I'd appreciate it if you would give them my card," she said as she handed one to Eileen.

"What is involved with being an apartment manager?" Eileen asked out of curiosity.

"It primarily involves collecting rents and scheduling maintenance on the apartments as tenants find problems. It also requires scheduling cleanup crews when someone vacates and acting as a rental agent for the company when apartments are available. Are you interested?"

"I don't think so," Eileen replied, slipping the card in her pocket. "I have a good job as the county school superintendent's assistant and I can't afford to leave it right now."

"You wouldn't have to," the manager said. "The job can normally be done in the evenings and weekends. It's really not a full-time position."

"Oh," Eileen said with new interest. "What does it pay?"

"We provide an apartment and all utilities, plus mileage if you have to use your car."

"I'm not sure I would be qualified. I've never even lived in an apartment until recently."

"I'd really rather train my managers myself," the manager said in response. "All I need is someone who is honest and willing to learn."

"That I am," Eileen said enthusiastically. "And I am very good at scheduling. I handle the scheduling of all the maintenance crews for the county school system now and thoroughly enjoy it."

"It sounds as if you could handle the job then. Why don't you come by my office tomorrow and fill out an application. I'll need to run a background check on you, but that's routine."

"I'll be by tomorrow after work. Would 4:30 be all right?"

"That'll be fine. I'll be looking for you."

The next day Eileen filled out the application for apartment manager. She was hired three days later and she and her family moved into a four-bedroom apartment, with all expenses paid. She turned out to be the best apartment manager the company had and often helped to train other new managers.

Her husband eventually filed for divorce in Texas, where he had relocated with the other woman, who also had divorced her husband. That marriage lasted less than two years—until she ran off with still another man.

Another idea that single parents have found to help their living expenses is to become live-in companions. There are many elderly people throughout our society who would like to be able to remain in their own homes, rather than go to a retirement home or live with their children. Most would be able to if they had someone living with them who could keep the home cleaned, cook some meals for them, and help them with periodic transportation. Several single parents I have known had their housing needs met in this manner. They're a help to the elderly, in return for living in their home.

The obvious potential for conflict requires that both parties be compatible and honest up front. Sometimes this arrangement doesn't work because of a clash of personalities, but very often it does, with all parties benefiting—especially the children, who benefit from the association with an older person. If children are to learn respect for the elderly in our society, they must be in close association with them.

A PRINCIPLE TO REMEMBER
Combining efforts and funds can benefit two people in need.

"Two are better than one because they have a good return for their labor" (Ecclesiastes 4:9).

TERRIBLE TRANSPORTATION

In our mobile society an automobile is no longer a luxury, it's a necessity—except in large metropolitan areas where public transportation is available. The cost of maintaining and operating a car is enormous for the majority of us. For a single parent living on a less than adequate income, that cost is a budget buster.

The constant fear of the car breaking down, and the helpless feeling when it does, often tempts the single mother to purchase a new car. Attracted by rebates and a low interest rate, many single parents will finance a new car that will totally wreck their budgets. The average family will spend about 15 to 18 percent of their disposable income buying a medium-priced new car.

Single parents, making about half the income of the average family, will spend upward of 25 to 30 percent. If they do, there is virtually no way their budgets will ever balance. A common plea among single parents who ask for help is, "How can I get rid of this car I bought, when it's not worth what I still owe on it?"

They end up selling the car at a loss, then paying the balance on a car they don't even own anymore. And what's worse, they don't even have their original car because they used it as a trade-in on the new one.

No matter what happens to your old car, it is almost always cheaper to repair the one you own than it is to purchase a new one. You should never commit more than 15 to 16 percent of your disposable income to transportation. This percentage includes payments, maintenance, gasoline, insurance, and so on.

So before you buy a new car, just calculate your Net Spendable Income (after tithes and taxes), multiply it by .16, and that is the total your budget can handle. For a single parent making $18,000 per year, the average net per month is $1,125. Thus the total amount that can be allocated to transportation is approximately $180 per month. A new car simply doesn't compute for most people. If, like Eileen, you have no expenses for housing or some other category of your budget, then you may be able to allocate more for transportation.

What are your alternatives? If you find that you must replace an older car, just remember that a good used car is significantly less expensive than a new one. If you want to calculate the loss in a new car after one year, a good rule of thumb is one-half of the original sticker price. That's a lot of depreciation when you consider it's probably half of the average single parent's income for a year!

The first logical alternative is to keep your old car going for as long as possible. Two factors usually work against the single parent trying to maintain an older car. First is the difficulty of locating a reliable, honest garage, with a mechanic who can repair an older car once it breaks down.

Second is the fact that most single parents, especially women, don't have the funds to keep their cars in good repair anyway and they allow them to deteriorate until several major breakdowns occur within a short period of time. This would be discouraging to anyone, but to a single mom it becomes a nightmare. Often she faces a several hundred dollar repair bill on a car that is probably worth less than the total cost of repairs.

I can almost hear some of the single parents reading this book saying, "Well, you hit the problem right on the head. But what can we do about it?" Individually there is not a lot you can do about it but, collectively, we can help solve the problem. A good friend, whom I'll call Terry, shared a similar situation that happened in his church.

Lee Ennis, the pastor of Terry's church, was counseling with several of the single parents in his congregation, and the transportation problem kept recurring so regularly that he felt the church had to do something to help. One solution was to help with the cost of their car repairs, and he often did so out of his own funds. But in a few months he realized this was just dealing with the symptom, not the real problem. By the time the women came for help, their cars had virtually disintegrated from lack of maintenance, and the repair costs were overwhelming.

For instance, usually these women had driven their cars on bad brakes long after the initial scraping sounds were first heard, sometimes until the car would no longer stop! By then the rotors or brake drums were badly scored and required replacing. So what might have initially been a $60 to $80 expense was now a $300 repair job!

After praying about the problem with his staff, the pastor called Terry and asked his opinion. Terry owned a large home building firm

and was known to have a good working knowledge of car maintenance. He regularly restored old cars as a hobby and had become the
resident counselor on car problems in the church.

"Terry, this is Lee. I really need your advice on something. Could
we have lunch on Tuesday?"

"Sure, Lee. Tuesday's fine. I'll pick you up." Terry knew the pastor
well enough to realize that when he called, asking for help, it was usually a major problem.

The next Tuesday, Terry and Pastor Lee met for lunch and the
pastor outlined the problem.

"The difficulty is, by the time we get a chance to see these
women, the problems are already out of hand. We would like to help
if possible. Any ideas?"

"Not right off hand, Lee. But give me a couple of days to think
about it. Maybe the Lord will give me an idea."

After the luncheon Terry did a lot of thinking and praying about
the problem. He discussed it with his wife that evening at dinner.

"Why don't we have the same problems with our cars that single
mothers do?" his wife Brenda asked, after he outlined what he and the
pastor discussed.

"Well, we do," Terry said as he thought about it. "Everybody does
if they have a car with over 20,000 miles on it. But I either fix the
problems myself or put the car right in the shop and have it fixed
before it gets any worse."

"Why don't single mothers do the same thing then?" Brenda
asked.

"Because they either don't recognize the problem or they don't
know where to take it," Terry replied as he thought back to his conversation with Pastor Ennis. "And many of them don't have the
money for car repair."

"Well you know a lot about cars, Terry. Why don't you just have
them call you when they think they have a problem. That's what I
do."

"I couldn't handle all the calls I would probably get," Terry said
hastily. "I would never get any work done."

"Then why don't you schedule a time when you would be willing
to help them?" Brenda asked. To her it seemed like a workable solution.

"I wouldn't be able to see all of them even if I set aside a day a week," Terry replied.

"Maybe there are some other men in the church who would be willing to help," Brenda suggested in her matter-of-fact manner. "Why not try it?"

The more Terry thought about Brenda's suggestion, the more he decided it had some merit. The next day he called Pastor Ennis and explained his plan.

"Lee, I'll mention the idea at our men's prayer breakfast this week. You tell the single mothers that you and your staff are counseling that they can have a free car checkup the first Saturday of each month in the church parking lot. Just have them sign up with your secretary and then let me know how many will be coming."

"Great idea, Terry. I'll get right on it," Lee said. He felt like a weight had been lifted off his shoulders.

The first Saturday three single mothers showed up to have their cars checked. Two of the vehicles had major problems that needed immediate work. Terry arranged with a garage to do the work and bill the women at whatever their counselor said they could afford. What they didn't know was that Terry paid the difference himself.

As the word spread in the church, more women asked for help with their cars, until Terry could no longer handle the load himself. By that time he had two other men who had volunteered to help. Each woman that wanted to bring her car was required to see a church counselor for a referral.

By the fourth month Terry had six volunteers working on alternate Saturdays. They not only would check out the cars, but they would do minor maintenance, such as oil changes, brake repairs, and tune-ups—to the extent their expertise would allow.

As the word spread outside the church, through women telling about it at work and other places, the church became like a magnet for single parents. Soon it was obvious to Terry that this could be a real area of ministry, both to the single parents in his church and also to many unsaved women who desperately needed help.

He had another idea: "I would like to propose that we buy the gas station on Main Street that went out of business and convert it into a car repair shop," Terry suggested at the volunteer staff's Monday morning meeting. "We could hire a mechanic to do minor repairs full-time and help check out the cars on Saturdays, like we have been doing. I also suggest that we charge whatever the counselor says these women can afford and subsidize the difference through our benevolence fund."

"Won't that get to be pretty expensive?" one of the other volunteers asked.

"If we have the entire men's group behind it, the total cost would be less than $50 a month each. As the word gets out, I believe we'll have some others who would help also," Terry said as he sat back down.

After deliberating the idea for a few minutes, the men prayed about it and then voted unanimously to adopt the car repair center as a group project.

The church now has nearly two hundred single parents signed up for the car helps ministry, many of whom became Christians as a result of one man's commitment to help solve a problem.

Unfortunately, this option is not available to most single parents, so they have to use other ideas. One idea available to most people is to buy a used car rather than a new one. The objection that many single women have to buying a used car is that they don't know how to tell a good one from a bad one. In reality, the same problem exists when buying a new car too. Remember that all those used cars were once new. So the lemons were out there from the beginning, only at a higher price. There are some steps you can take to lessen the risk when buying a used car.

1. Get help. Almost always there are men (and women) within a church who have a very good understanding of automobiles. I have found that most people are glad to help another person evaluate a potential car, once they have narrowed down the search a little. Don't be hesitant to ask for help. The only way these people can exercise the gifts and abilities God has given them is for others to ask.

2. Check it out. The one thing you can count on is that a poorly made new car doesn't get better with age. Magazines such as *Consumer Reports* evaluate all new automobiles. If, for instance, you are considering a two-year-old Oldsmobile, go to the library and check a copy of the magazine in the year the car was originally sold. If it was graded a poor car when it was new, avoid it. It may be cheaper, but it may cost more in the long run.

3. Check the warranty.. Many late model used cars carry a transferable warranty that may be good for up to 50,000 miles or more. If you have a concern about the potential cost of maintenance, these warranties usually cover the major power train items, which are the most expensive to repair. If you have a question about what the warranty will or will not cover, call the manufacturer.

Sometimes a dealer will offer a dealership extended warranty on the car you buy. Be sure you have someone who knows contracts check it out very carefully. My personal experience has been that they exclude more than they cover.

THE BEST SOURCES FOR USED CARS

In talking with many people who buy and sell cars, I have found some common points of agreement in locating the best buys for the money. These certainly are not absolutes, but they are a reliable guide when looking for a good used automobile.

1. Check with friends and family first. Often you will be able to locate the best value by asking around your church to see if anyone has a dependable car for sale. Most people are basically honest and will tell you the truth about their cars. This is particularly important if a car has more than 30,000 miles on it.

A second benefit is that sometimes they will self-finance all or a portion of the cost, which saves a great deal on interest. And in most states the sale of a private individual's car is not subject to sales taxes, which again translates into savings for you.

2. Shop the local newspaper or auto trader paper. If you are unable to locate the right car through friends or family, the next best source is classified advertisements. Often people who buy new cars will elect to sell their used cars themselves. As I said before, most people are basically honest and will tell you the real condition of their car, if you ask them the right questions: Has it ever been in an accident? Has it been a low or a high maintenance car? Have teenagers driven it regularly? Did you buy it new? (I'd rarely buy a second- or third-owner car.) How often was the oil changed?

3. Visit dealerships. This is the most common source that used car buyers frequent because dealers are easily available, they arrange financing, and they always have a supply of cars available. Remember that they also must mark up their cars to make a profit so, unless you know the owner by reputation, they may not always be as truthful as other sources.

4. Try a wholesaler. Wholesalers are car auctions where used cars are regularly sold. But unless you know a great deal about cars, I would suggest that you stay away from wholesale auctions. The low prices tend to attract many nonprofessional buyers, but often they are unpleasantly surprised. Even though some very nice cars pass through auctions, they are also places where dealers dump their worst cars. You may be buying the proverbial "pig in a poke."

A PRINCIPLE TO REMEMBER

Ask for help when you have a need.

"Without consultation, plans are frustrated, but with many counselors they succeed" (Proverbs 15:22).

CHILD CARE COSTS

When our children were young, my wife Judy had the option to work at home or in an office. She opted to work at home until our youngest went off to college. That is an option most single parents don't have in this generation. Unless they are willing to live on welfare, at less than poverty income, they must work, usually outside the home.

I have heard all the arguments for and against single parents working, especially mothers with small children. I can honestly say I don't know how they cope. Even with both husband and wife sharing the burden, it is difficult. But a working single mother with small children lives in a state of near emotional and physical exhaustion, unless she has some unusual circumstances.

Combine this with the financial pressures of child care and it is easy to see why many single parents jump into another bad living arrangement that they often regret. It's called desperation.

The cost of child care won't compute in the average family's budget. On an income of $24,000 a year, daily child care consumes nearly 13 percent of disposable income (about $2,100 to $2,400 per year). That amount simply cannot be worked into the normal family's budget and still leave funds for vacations, entertainment, eating out, and the like. But since the child care is a by-product of the working wife, they have her income to do these things. So, in reality, she ends up working to support the child care center and family activities that are necessitated because of the pressures created by a working mother. As a counselor I realize it's not really that simple, but it often seems that way to me when couples outline their problems.

If the cost of child care won't compute in the average family's budget, it certainly won't compute in a single parent's more limited budget. Unfortunately it must! Child care for one preschooler runs about $325 per month in most parts of the country (higher in metro areas). For two children (the norm in most single parent families), it runs about $450 per month. That equates to about 30 to 40 percent of most single parents' disposable income. Is it any wonder why we have so many latchkey kids in America? As soon as children are old enough to know not to burn the house down while they are home alone, they are on their own.

Adding to the guilt of parking a child in a day care center, or in a private home, is the knowledge that most of them are being fed a constant diet of sex and violence through the television several hours each day. It's no wonder that we're having drug, sex, and suicide problems with our younger generation. By the time most of them are in their early teens, they have had more adult experiences than an average 30 year old of two generations ago.

It's easy to put a guilt trip on single parents because they spend so little time with their children. Single parents love their children just as much as the average couple does. But what are the alternatives available to them? In reality, very few—without help from outside. The resources are available to solve this problem, but they are not in the hands of single parents. They are within the churches of America.

Unfortunately, as of this writing, the churches of America have not taken the lead in helping to solve the dilemma. As a result, the federal government has stepped in with a child care program that will increase taxes and still not solve the problem. It amazes me that taxpayers can be tricked into believing that the government can take a bad system and make it a winner by pouring more money into it.

An education system that can't teach a child how to read and write in twelve years of study says it needs the children at a younger age, and they need more money to do the job. A welfare system that consumes over 80 percent of allocated funds in administrative overhead thinks it can administer child care centers better than private individuals. The cost to the single parents will go down, but the cost to the taxpayers will escalate out of control.

I don't fault the single parents for wanting the child care legislation—they need help. It's the church in America that has failed in its responsibility to help the poor among us. As a result, many more Americans now look to the government as their source of aid, rather than looking to God. The solution is available; all it takes is caring Christians.

A few years back I met a single parent who had made a difference in her church in the area of child care for working single parents. Pam had been a Christian for nearly three years when her husband Cal decided he'd had enough of religion and told her he wanted a divorce.

"I just don't want to live with a religious fanatic," Cal said in response to Pam's question about why he wanted a divorce.

"But have I tried to force Christianity on you?" Pam asked as she tried to cope with Cal's attitude.

"Maybe not, but you sit around reading that stupid Bible all the time. I want to have some fun in life. I don't want to live with some saint."

"But Cal, I'm not trying to be a saint," Pam protested. "I didn't know my Bible study bothered you. I would be glad to do it when you're not here if it offends you."

"No, that's just a part of it, Pam. We have different friends now. I don't feel like bringing my friends over here because they don't go to church either. And I know you're not going drinking with us anymore."

"I don't have the desire to drink anymore, Cal. But that doesn't mean I don't love you. It's just that Jesus Christ is the center of my life now and I don't need to drink."

"See what I mean?" Cal shouted as he stormed out of the room. "You don't need to drink! Well neither do I! I do it because I like to!"

This scene was repeated often over the next several months until, ultimately, Cal packed up and left. He provided Pam with about $500 a month, obviously inadequate for her needs with three children from ages 3 to 12.

Pam began a search for a job that would at least meet her minimum needs. She ended up as a clerk for an insurance company, making about $1,000 a month. With two children in school she had only the three-year-old son to place in day care. But as she shopped for a good day care center, she quickly found that the average fee of $325 a month was still pushing her budget to the limit. For her older two, it meant that the 12-year-old became the baby sitter for nearly two hours a day, until Pam returned home—often to find a raging war of wills going on between the two girls. She could see summer break coming and had no idea how she would handle that situation.

In the meantime Cal filed for divorce and it was granted. The judge assigned child support of $375 a month. Suddenly Pam found herself with a financial deficit each month, as the expenses exceeded her income. She made the necessary adjustments, which included eliminating any clothing budget, car maintenance, or eating out. Still her budget was tight, and she knew it was just a matter of time until it collapsed.

In the meantime she was having to deal with an entirely new problem. Her pastor called and asked if she would come by his office. She agreed and set up an appointment for that Friday.

Pam pondered all week what he might want of her. *Perhaps he wants to know if we have any needs,* she thought. *It is a caring church that ministers to some of the poor in the community.* When she arrived at the church office, the secretary showed her into the pastor's study. There was another couple already there. Pam recognized the man as being the chairman of the board of deacons. The lady was his wife and head of the women's missionary society.

The pastor said, "Pam, I hope you'll take this the right way, but the church has decided to suspend your membership."

"What! But why?" Pam nearly shouted in her shock.

"Because we believe that divorce is a sin. Therefore, you're living in sin and cannot hold your membership."

"But I didn't divorce my husband," Pam protested. "He divorced me. I wouldn't even agree to the divorce. But in this state either spouse can get a divorce if the judge agrees."

"That may be," the woman said curtly. "But we also understand you have been talking about what happened with your Sunday school class. Is that right?"

"Well, yes," Pam admitted. "But I wasn't encouraging anyone else to get a divorce. I was sharing how difficult it is to be a single parent in our society."

"If you were truly innocent, you wouldn't be having financial problems," the pastor commented. "It is our belief that God is using this because you have hidden sins in your life."

"And we don't want to give others the idea that they can get divorced with no consequences," the woman added.

"You can still attend the church, Pam. But you won't be able to take communion or vote in church matters," the pastor said, looking at the floor.

"And you won't be allowed to speak up in Sunday school," the deacon chimed in. "You need to accept this as God's judgment, Pam, and repent of whatever is wrong in your life."

Pam sat there stunned; she couldn't even defend herself. As the tears formed in her eyes, she stood up and walked out of the room. On her way home she got more and more angry. All kinds of thoughts crossed her mind, from suing the church to addressing the next Sunday service. But as she calmed down a bit, she realized that neither was right, according to God's Word. *I just won't allow them to drag me down to their level,* Pam decided resolutely. The next Sunday she went out looking for a new church home.

Within a few weeks she had found a church in which she felt very comfortable, and she and the children were attending regularly. One evening her doorbell rang and when she opened the door, she was surprised to see the pastor of the new church.

He introduced himself. "I'm Pastor Ross. I know you and your family have been attending our church, and I just wanted to drop by and welcome you."

Pam thanked him and then told him about her recent divorce and asked about the church's policy toward divorcees joining the church.

"We're a church made up of forgiven sinners," the pastor said. "If you know the Lord, that's our only requirement. We do require that all prospective members attend an orientation class before joining, but that is only to ensure that they all understand the plan of salvation first."

Pam joined the church and got involved in their single parents' ministry. Some months later, at one of the evening meetings, the subject of child care came up. Several of the single parents shared their dilemma of inadequate care for their children and their concern over the influence their children received at a secular facility. Several commented about the rock music that was played all day. A woman shared that at one center the attendant watched pornographic videos during nap times. She learned about it from her three-year-old who uttered a few four-letter words.

Over the next several meetings an idea jelled. Why doesn't the church sponsor a day care center for members that would be staffed by one full-time person and volunteers? It was agreed that the idea would be presented to the pastor.

Pastor Ross agreed wholeheartedly, and the child care center was born. Within six months all the necessary support had been raised, the necessary permits were obtained, and Pam had organized twelve women to assist the director, a Christian who had been hired from a local facility.

The day care center struggled along on limited funds for several months. Many of the mothers who applied for their children to attend were turned away, including Pam, because of the lack of resources. Just when it seemed that the idea would fall apart, Pam received a call one evening from a member who owned a large contracting firm in the city.

"Pam, I heard about your efforts to start a child care center at the church. The pastor said that it appears you'll have to shut it down. Is that right?"

"That's the way it looks," Pam said as she took a deep breath. She had not even admitted that inevitable prospect to herself. But the truth was, they had not been able to pay the director her full salary for nearly two months now. The single parents just couldn't pay enough to get the center established.

"I understand some of the problems that single mothers are facing," he said. "My own daughter is in that same situation, and if it weren't for our help each month she couldn't make it. Her husband has taken off and nobody knows where he is."

I know the feeling, Pam thought to herself. *Half the single parents in our group don't get any support from their husbands.*

"I'd like to help, if it's okay," the man said. "I'd like to make a gift to the center for the next couple of years."

"That would really help," Pam responded, not having any idea if he was talking about a gift of $100 or $1,000.

Two days later the pastor called to tell her that the gift to the center had arrived by mail. It was for $50,000! Over the next two years the church day care center for single parents expanded to take care of nearly sixty children, including a summer program for latchkey kids.

The program still functions on a can-pay basis, with all participants required to attend financial counseling sessions in the church. Most of the volunteer help now comes from mothers with husbands who want to help the single parents and from older members who have free time available.

The church also has organized a mentoring ministry to help the children of single parents have an opposite-sex influence in their lives. They organize field trips, fishing and hiking outings, and a variety of other activities that most of these kids would otherwise miss out on.

Another single parent tackled the child care problem in a different way. Lori came from an abusive family. Her father left when she was a little girl. Her mother worked and left Lori in child care. It was there that she was molested by a child care worker. With no one left in her life to reaffirm her identity, her self-image was shattered. As a teen she found herself in several destructive dating relationships and eventually entered into an abusive marriage. When her husband left her, she decided to give up on men and focus on herself and her children.

With no other resources available to her, she reluctantly put her children in day care. She earned a degree in early childhood education and went to work in the county children's services department. Her job was to train child care providers. Due to her own experiences, she focused on accountability and credibility.

Even with the government job, Lori struggled to meet the monthly expense of two preschoolers in day care. She was continually worried about the day care environment and wanted to be home with her children. Training had even become difficult because she found herself disagreeing with much of the material she was required to teach. She knew she wouldn't be able to continue much longer.

Lori's perspective first began to change after meeting a Christian couple who had invited her to their church. She began attending and eventually accepted the Lord into her life. Through the women in the church's single parents' group, she began to realize that other single parents struggled with the cost and dangers of child care as much as she did. Lori had an inspiration to train Christian in-home care providers, but as a low-income single mom herself she didn't know where to begin.

She took her ideas to the church's singles pastor, who had helped develop in his former church a highly successful single parent ministry that included a day care. Since Lori had the training and background, he strongly encouraged her to pursue establishing child care training. Together, they developed a plan for Lori to fill the need.

In her state, child care providers have to be licensed, even if they only care for one child that is not a relative. Lori found married, stay-at-home mothers, who were willing to become licensed and offer Christian in-home care. She has been in business for over a year now and has fifty child care homes established in her community. Each home has five to six children from married and single parent households to care for. They offer hot meals, outings, and preschool activities. Single parents pay a sliding scale fee, based on what they can afford. Couples generally pay full price. The church takes an offering once a quarter to help cover single parents' expenses.

Lori supports herself with the income from training and overseeing the providers. Although it is still a struggle financially, she was thrilled to be able to stay at home with her two children for the last year. The oldest will be entering first grade next year. Plus, there's another bonus to her new endeavor.

Through encouraging friendships and working relationships she has developed with male Christians, Lori has changed her perception about relationships and dating. She now says that some day she may even get married.

All it takes is the commitment of one individual to marshal the troops that God has already equipped. Pam and Lori were willing to be used to help solve a problem they faced.

A PRINCIPLE TO REMEMBER
Don't judge others; help them.

"For the whole Law is fulfilled in one word, in the statement, 'You shall love your neighbor as yourself.' But if you bite and devour one another, take care lest you be consumed by one another" (Galatians 5:14-15).

Chapter 9

ALIMONY, CHILD SUPPORT, AND LAWSUITS

Single parents are faced with some difficult decisions:

- Should I ask for alimony?
- Should I keep the home?
- Should I take a lump sum settlement?
- Should I sue for failure to pay?
- Should I sue for future increases?

These are not easy decisions for anyone. But for Christians, the decisions are even more confusing. In addition to weighing traditional wisdom, Christians also must weigh the counsel of God's Word. That wouldn't be difficult if the counsel were absolute: Do not sue, do not hold the other parent accountable for his or her children's expenses, and so on.

Unfortunately, God's Word is not clear on this subject and usually requires some interpretation. Furthermore, the interpretation you get often depends on who is doing the interpreting.

A counselor who relates primarily to married couples will almost always say, "Wives, obey your husbands that you may win them over."

A counselor who deals with battered women or abused children usually will say, "Call the police and have him thrown in jail."

A counselor who deals with abandoned families, usually single mothers, often will say, "Sue him for support, and throw him in jail if he doesn't pay."

Virtually every one of these Christian counselors believes in what he or she says and does. However, each is looking from a biased perspective. They are greatly influenced by the clients they see and the misery they share. I can understand that. Often I have felt the same way with people I have counseled. I empathized with them, as any caring person will do.

Perhaps if I had been alive in the Lord's day and had been a disciple, I might have been tempted to raise a group of zealots and try to rescue Jesus from the Jews. But I rather suspect that if one of Jesus' followers had attempted to do that, he would have been chastened, just as the Lord chastened Peter for resisting the mob that came for Him. It's important to remember: *Man's way is not God's way.*

Good counselors must learn to disassociate themselves from their own feelings and give counsel that is based on the best interpretation of God's Word. Many times I have listened while honest, dedicated Christians explained how other Christians they trusted had willfully cheated them and several others out of their money. Often, after persistent efforts to get the issue resolved, the offender simply said, "So if you don't like it, sue me."

Almost always the counselees in my office were there asking if they could do exactly that: sue the guilty spouse. They usually had already received the go-ahead from one or more other counselors, sometimes including their pastor. Emotionally I agree with the logic of suing a crook, Christian or not, who refuses all attempts to amiably settle the issue. Almost certainly these people are going to cheat someone else in the future.

But the issue isn't what I think or what any other counselor thinks; it's what God thinks! Sometimes, when the answer is not clear, several counselors are required. *"Without consultation, plans are frustrated, but with many counselors they succeed"* (Proverbs 15:22).

However, when the issue is not in doubt, only one source of counsel is required, according to Proverbs 8:10, *"Take my instruction, and not silver, and knowledge rather than choicest gold."*

I recall an incident from several years ago that helped to solidify in my own mind that God's Word is the ultimate source of all decisions.

Jean was going through a bitter divorce. Her husband Rex had left her for a younger woman. I knew Rex from several men's Bible studies I had attended shortly after becoming a Christian. He was an able teacher, and I had learned a great deal under his teaching. The only potential flaw I noticed was that he was overzealous about Christianity. He set Sundays aside, for his whole family, as a day dedicated to nothing but studying the Word.

Although there is nothing wrong with that, he seemed to attack his faith as an effort in pleasing God, rather than serving Him. His messages were heavy with the need to sacrifice for the Lord, and he commented that if Christians didn't spend at least an hour a day in prayer they were not dedicated. Although I couldn't deny that what he was saying made a lot of sense, both practically and biblically, I felt he was trying to earn God's favor. I figured that if it didn't work for the Pharisees I probably didn't have a chance; so, I accepted the majority of his teaching and just ignored the legalistic side.

When Rex left his family and filed for divorce, Jean had been advised by several other Christians to "make it tough" on Rex. He was trying to take virtually all their household items, including the furniture, their best car, a nice boat, and several other items that were needed by Jean and their three children.

They had operated a business together for several years, and he wanted to buy out her interest, using proceeds from the business to do so (not a great deal for Jean).

Jean's question was a very honest and basic one: "Should I hold out for as much as I can get (and probably have a right to)?"

There seemed to be no doubt that the marriage was over. Rex was currently living with the younger woman and had expressed his desire to marry her as soon as possible. If anyone ever had a biblical right to divorce her husband, it was Jean. And it certainly didn't make any sense not to secure her own future since Rex had made it clear he did not intend to do so.

I really didn't know how to counsel Jean at the time. Somewhere in my mind there was a nagging feeling that Jesus probably would have told her not to hold out for all she could get. I also had a doubt that He would have advised her to countersue for divorce, as she had been advised. But my emotions told me that Rex was a self-centered hypocrite, who simply dumped her for a newer model. I asked her to give me a day to pray about what counsel I could offer.

That night I spent some time in prayer, just asking the Lord to give me the wisdom He had promised (see James 1:5). By the next morning I knew I had the answer God intended for me—and hopefully for Jean.

When we met the next day, I shared with her what I knew from God's Word about the relationship between a husband and wife. One of the first examples we have is that of Abram and Sarai in Genesis 12. Abram tried to trade Sarai to the Pharaoh because he feared for himself. Through it all she honored her husband and later was blessed by God. As you probably know, later Abraham did the same thing again.

In Ephesians 5, Paul gives the primary teaching in the New Testament on husband and wife relationships. I have heard teachers say that the instructions given in Ephesians 5 are conditional, meaning the wife should do her part only if her husband does his part. I can find no such condition in all the Bible. Marriage is a vow taken by two people to unconditionally love each other.

God doesn't make any of the marriage instructions conditional. Each spouse is totally responsible to do what God says, regardless of whether the other one obeys. Each of us will be accountable for our own actions when we stand before the Lord. I find this interpretation makes my decisions a lot easier when sorting them out.

We ended the session in Philippians 2:3, where Paul said, *"Do nothing from selfishness or empty conceit, but with humility of mind let each of you regard one another as more important than himself,"* and in Philippians 3:8, where he said, *"More than that, I count all things to be loss in view of the surpassing value of knowing Christ Jesus my Lord, for whom I have suffered the loss of all things, and count them but rubbish in order that I may gain Christ."* I closed by asking Jean to pray about these passages and then do as she felt the Lord was leading her.

The next day she called to say that what we had discussed confirmed what she had been feeling all along. She would not countersue and would not fight Rex for any properties. She would rely on the Lord to do the convicting for her.

I received a couple of heated calls about the "advice" I had given her. The pastor challenged my ability to give good counsel to anyone. "If that's the kind of advice you give," he said sternly, "I would suggest you keep it to yourself." The second caller, her attorney, issued a slightly veiled threat that if she regretted the decision later I might be held liable for the advice I gave.

I explained to both of them that I had not given advice at all. My counsel was given to help her reach the decision that she felt was from the Lord. If they had a problem with that, they should take it up with Him.

I would like to be able to say that every time a Christian decides to trust God and do exactly what His Word says it works out for his or her good. I do believe that ultimately it will, but it may be in the next lifetime, not this one. The issue is not gratification in the human sense. It is obedience to our Lord.

In Daniel 3, Shadrach, Meshach, and Abed-nego told Nebuchadnezzar that if he threw them into his furnace their God could rescue them from it. But then they made it clear that even if He didn't rescue them, they would not bow to his idol. They were being obedient.

Jean's attorney did everything he could to talk her out of her decision, as did her pastor and several close friends. They resented the idea that Rex might get away with his scheme. Jean called me a couple of times when her resolve was low, typically after she had some dealings with Rex and his attitude was particularly rotten.

During one such call I told her what I believed to be the truth: "Jean, if your decision is based on expecting Rex to change, then you probably have made the wrong choice. He may never change, but that's his problem. Your decision must be based on a conviction from the Lord, not that of a counselor—me or anyone else."

One of the things I have learned by experience is that all counselors are wrong sometimes; some are wrong most of the time. The Proverbs give a good balance to remember when seeking counsel. First, *"Without consultation, plans are frustrated, but with many counselors they succeed"* (Proverbs 15:22). This indicates that a wise person seeks the counsel of others before making critical decisions. Second, *"The naive believes everything, but the prudent man considers his steps"*

(Proverbs 14:15). This indicates that only fools listen to most of what they hear.

At first Rex thought Jean was pulling some kind of ploy on him, so he instructed his attorney to ask for even more concessions, one of which was no alimony. Jean agreed. The only stipulation she gave was that Rex must provide child support for his children. Jean had her resolve tested many times during the next several months. When Rex came by to see the children, she treated him like a friend that had dropped by to visit. No matter what he did, she tried not to react negatively.

Then one day Rex called unexpectedly and asked if he could come by. Jean agreed, and later that day he arrived. She had made some coffee and asked him to come into the kitchen.

She had just poured the coffee when Rex said, "Jean, I would like to come home."

Jean almost dropped the coffee cup she was holding. Instead she took a sip and calmly asked, "Why?"

"Because I know how wrong I've been. I've been living in sin and I can't stand myself anymore. I've already been to the pastor and asked for forgiveness. I've agreed to apologize before the church and enter the new members' class."

Jean literally gulped down the scalding coffee as her heart thumped. "Are you sure this is what you want, Rex?"

"I've never been so sure of anything, but I wouldn't blame you if you said no. I'll sleep on the couch if you want. You've been so great about this and I've been a louse."

"I can't disagree," Jean said with a smile, "but I'm willing to try if you are."

It has now been nearly ten years since the incident with Rex and Jean. They are still married and Rex has been the model of a dedicated husband. He has refused any additional leadership within the church and limits himself to counseling men who have left their families. Jean didn't really win Rex back; God did.

In a divorce, you must ultimately decide for yourself about the settlement and whether to fight for your rights. There are few, if any, biblical principles to guide you in these decisions simply because God doesn't prescribe rules for dissolving a marriage.

It is my personal conviction that a man is responsible for his family, including his spouse. That responsibility doesn't end simply because the law says they are no longer married. But once either party remarries and it is no longer possible to restore the relationship, that line of authority ceases. The wife is free from his authority. However, the husband is still biblically responsible for his children.

On the other side of the support issue, there are a growing number of fathers raising children who receive little or no support—emotionally, physically, or spiritually—from their children's mother. Even though the father is generally considered the provider, the mother still has a responsibility to provide loving care for her children.

SHOULD YOU DEMAND THE HOME?

Often women in the midst of a divorce cling to their homes for security. In reality, the home can be a financial weight that pulls them down. The decision to keep or sell a home should be based on a budget, not emotions. If sufficient funds are available to maintain the home for a period of time after the divorce, generally that is a matter of choice.

There is always the chance that the marriage will be restored. But I have seen many divorcees literally impoverished by trying to maintain a home far beyond their budgets. The pressure to maintain the previous lifestyle for the children is usually the motivation. Second to that is the idea that the home represents security for the future—that buying another home later will be impossible.

In the next chapters we will be looking at some rules of budgeting for single parents, one of which is, make the hard decisions quickly so they don't become impossible decisions later. If you are spending more than approximately 40 percent of your disposable income (Net Spendable Income), it probably will have to go!

Candy was in the midst of a divorce that had devastated her. She and David had been married since their second year in college and, although theirs was a stormy relationship, she had never seriously thought about a divorce. Both had good jobs in the same bank. Candy was the assistant marketing director, a job high in prestige but low in pay.

They lived in a very nice home that both had contributed a lot of time and effort toward—so much so that Candy hadn't noticed the little telltale signs of David's involvement with someone else. It was only when David decided to leave that she realized he had been seeing another bank employee for nearly a year.

They had two children: a son in high school and another in junior high. As the divorce proceeded and Candy realized that David was not coming back, she clung to her home as the last sense of security. The difficulty was that to maintain the payments required two incomes. At the court hearing David agreed to pay $500 a month child support and six months' alimony of $500.

Unfortunately, this was enough to tempt Candy into trying to keep the home. She rationalized the decision as an effort to stabilize her children after the trauma of the divorce and subsequent remarriage of their father.

Within a year Candy was hopelessly in debt. She had borrowed against the equity in the home to keep the payments current for the first several months. Then, in an effort to extend the inevitable a little longer, she attempted to remortgage. If she had sold the home soon after the divorce, she could have recovered the equity of nearly $25,000. In the meantime the market had dropped, because of an oil-related recession in her area, and the home was worth less than the outstanding mortgages.

There was little any counselor could do, except negotiate with the lender for an orderly repossession. Fortunately, in her state the law prohibited surety for deficiencies on homes, so she was able to get out of the home debt-free. As the Lord said in Luke 14:28, it is important to sit down, consider the entire cost, and decide if you have enough funds to complete the task. Candy's decision was made the day David remarried; she was just unwilling to accept it then.

A LUMP SUM SETTLEMENT

Hope was offered a lump sum settlement through her husband's attorney. Brian was a surgeon earning over $200,000 a year. Based on his income, his attorney figured Hope was entitled to child support of $1,500 a month for their three children and alimony of $1,000 a month. Since Hope had worked for five years to help put Brian through college and medical school, her attorney also was asking for an additional settlement of $2,000 a month for five years.

Their relationship was a rocky one from the beginning. Brian was a workaholic and stayed away from home most of the time. They had started marriage on the wrong foot: Hope was pregnant. She had dropped out of nursing school just after they were married, and then she had a miscarriage and lost the baby. Almost immediately she went back to school and finished her training. Brian was a senior in premed and was dedicated to being a surgeon, like his father.

Throughout medical school, Hope worked and Brian spent long hours studying and interning. She complained that they never saw each other but always assumed that would eventually change when Brian finished school.

Instead, it got progressively worse. Once out of school Brian began his residency and then received a grant to study pediatric surgery in England. By this time they had one child, with another on the way, and Hope could not go with him. He commuted for nearly two years, seeing his family only once every two months at best. After his residency and certification, he accepted a position with a prestigious university hospital in the Washington, D.C. area and quickly rose to become the head of pediatric surgery.

Unfortunately, each successive step put Brian more out of touch with his family. Hope began to complain, and later to nag, about his lack of compassion for his children (and her). To a physician who receives nothing but accolades at work and admiration from his patients, too often the stress of a family drives him further into his work. This is exactly what happened to Brian. Finally he decided to move out of the house and into an apartment.

In Hope's words, "I hardly knew the difference and the kids didn't really know their father anyway." Quickly they moved apart, in what they both knew from the beginning probably would be a permanent situation. Hope had begun to drink heavily. Her mother was an alcoholic, and it frightened Hope to realize she might become one too. She finally went to her best friend Jenny for help. Jenny recommended that she talk with their pastor, who also was a recovering alcoholic.

During their first session together, Pastor Clemmons explained how he had become an alcoholic while running a psychological counseling business. As a trained psychologist, he knew the dangers of any drug, but a nagging fear of the future led him to drink to escape the depression that haunted him.

"That's just where I am," Hope confessed. "Brian and I got married for the wrong reasons and I know he doesn't really love me. I don't seem to fit into his world and he doesn't want to fit into mine."

Pastor Clemmons asked Hope to attend a helps class that he was teaching one night a week for people with dependency problems. After some initial struggles with admitting she had a problem, Hope agreed to attend. The deciding factor was her alarm at the realization that she could no longer fall asleep without having three or four drinks every night. The thought of an even greater dependency on alcohol frightened her into swallowing her pride.

Several weeks later, at one of the meetings, she committed her life to Christ and was delivered from her fears and dependency on alcohol.

Hope tried to share her experience with Brian over the next few weeks, but it was clear that he neither cared about nor shared her beliefs. He saw religion as just one more crutch needed by his weak-willed wife. His subsequent offer to settle the property side of their divorce was his way of closing that chapter in his life.

Hope knew that once their divorce was finalized Brian would buffer himself from her and the children and bury himself in his work. If he were released from any continuing responsibility, they quite likely would become victims of the old out-of-sight, out-of-mind syndrome.

She decided not to take the settlement of nearly $500,000. Instead she dropped her demands for alimony and requested that her child support be increased to $2,500 a month, which would allow her to pay for an in-home sitter while she worked. Brian's attorney jumped at the offer and pressured him into agreeing as quickly as possible.

Needless to say, Hope's attorney was distraught. She had traded a guaranteed income of at least $25,000 a year, plus child support, for $30,000 a year in child support for not longer than fifteen years (the age of maturity for their youngest child). Hope calmly explained her reasoning on the counsel of her new pastor: "Leave the door open for God to work."

The divorce was finalized and, true to form, Brian virtually severed all ties with his family. He would send them presents on their birthdays and at Christmas, but he seldom visited. Hope continued to grow in her faith, and the one thing that did impress Brian was her lack of dependence on him. She took a job as a night nurse at the same hospital where he practiced, and he would periodically hear reports from other nurses of her abilities and compassion. Twice she was offered a shift supervisor's position and turned it down so she could spend more time with her children.

She also had many opportunities to date hospital staff and turned them all down, saying that she still considered herself to be married, another comment that did not go unnoticed by Brian.

Three years after their divorce, an event took place that changed Brian's life. He was involved in a very bad automobile accident that left his right arm partially paralyzed from a back injury. Abruptly his career as a surgeon ended. He continued on as chief-of-staff but in a nonsurgical role. Suddenly, without the demands of an attending physician, he found himself with surplus time on his hands. For Brian, it was as if his meaning for life was gone. He felt like a charity case.

In the midst of all this he began looking for some answers. He turned to Hope for help. One evening he called and asked if he could come over to talk with her. She agreed.

"Hope, I just wanted to tell you that I have changed my will. I'm leaving everything to you and the kids," he said despondently.

"You sound like this is an epitaph," Hope said, sensing his words as those of a potential suicide.

"Maybe so," Brian replied. "I don't have anything left to live for. I messed up our marriage and now I'm no longer any good to anyone —at least not alive. Maybe my death will have some meaning; my life sure doesn't."

"I think you're about to make the biggest blunder so far," Hope said, looking him in the eyes.

"What do you mean?" Brian asked, astonished. This was a side of Hope he hadn't seen before. It was as if he were a student and she was his instructor.

"Brian, haven't you wondered what it is that has given me the strength to go through these last five years?" she asked.

"Well, I know there has been a change in you," he remarked. "I guess you mean it's your religion. That's okay for you. But it's not my thing."

"Religion isn't my thing, either—as you put it," she replied defensively. "I know the Creator of this world as my Savior. That's my strength and comfort. What do you have that carries you through the trials, Brian?"

"Nothing I guess," he replied. "My whole life seems a waste now."

"That's only because you allow it to. But if you think you have problems now, just think what it'll be like for eternity to realize that you made the biggest mistake of your life. You rejected the only person who can release you from your guilt and sins: the Lord Jesus Christ."

"That's okay for you, Hope. But I don't believe in God. When you die, you die—that's it."

"But what if you're wrong, Brian? Then what? Do you think you've been wrong about other things?"

"Probably so."

"Well, stop listening to the people around you who tell you how great you are because you're a doctor. We're all sinners and need help."

Hope and Brian had many more conversations like this one over the next several weeks. The evidence that Hope had piqued Brian's interest was that he didn't attempt suicide. He began to attend the helps group meetings from time to time and was impressed by the total honesty of the group and the fact that he could be himself without any pretense. Later that year Brian committed his life to Christ and began to mature spiritually.

The change was dramatic, and he attacked his newfound faith with the same vigor he had shown in his career as a physician. A few months later he and Hope were remarried. Brian accepted a position as head of a missions medical staff in Southeast Asia, where he and Hope now live. Their children are married to Christians, and each is serving in ministries throughout the world.

Certainly not all situations work out as well as Hope and Brian's. It is more common for marriages to fail and the families to be split forever. However, I believe the key ingredient in any marriage that survives is a total surrender to the Lord.

For divorcees facing the decision of whether to accept a lump sum settlement, it is important to make that decision on your own, based on God's counsel in your life. It will be different for everyone. In general, I counsel a prospective divorcee not to accept a lump sum settlement, unless there is a very realistic prospect that her husband will not support his family once the divorce is finalized.

The majority of women I have counseled who accepted lump sum settlements ended up either losing the money through bad investments or spending it during the first few years. Obviously, good money management helps to avoid these situations. But just as recent widows are vulnerable to outside influences, so are recent divorcees.

SHOULD YOU SUE FOR NONPAYMENT?

This is an issue that more and more single parents are facing in our society: Should you sue for nonpayment of alimony or child support? First, I would like to discuss the simpler issue of suing for nonpayment of alimony.

Alimony is the regular monthly support assigned to one spouse (more often the husband) for the support of the other spouse for a designated period of time. In the last decade or so it is less common for a spouse to receive alimony, except in cases in which an enormous income is at stake, such as the divorces of entertainers, athletes, and the like.

On the basis of God's Word, I can see nothing that would scripturally allow a single parent to sue a former spouse for nonpayment of alimony. I personally believe that a man should pay to support his former wife, since God doesn't recognize divorce. The same goes for the wife if she was the primary breadwinner. But if the departed spouse will not pay, the single parent still should not sue.

I know this counsel will run contrary to much Christian teaching, as I told you earlier that it would. I even humanly agree with the logic of suing sorry rascals who won't support their spouses. I also have seen, firsthand, the difficulties the lack of alimony can cause. But God's Word is not dependent on our human logic or approval. Just as the three Jewish disciples, whose story is told in Daniel 3, had to be willing to commit themselves to the furnace, so must a Christian, if he or she is ever to tap into the power of the Lord.

Sometimes the answer may not be what we would wish. Perhaps there were other young men throughout history who refused to bow and lost their lives. They are not recorded. Bear in mind the words of the Lord: *"Then Jesus said to His disciples, 'If anyone wishes to come after Me, let him deny himself, and take up his cross, and follow Me. For whoever wishes to save his life shall lose it; but whoever loses his life for My sake shall find it. For what will a man be profited, if he gains the whole world, and forfeits his soul? Or what will a man give in exchange for his soul?'"* (Matthew 16:24-26).

The issue of child support is an entirely different matter. Unlike the parents, children have no choice in their circumstances. They did not choose to be born to us. They were given to our care by God. Parents cannot refuse their responsibilities to their children just because it is inconvenient. As Paul said, *"But if anyone does not provide for his own, and especially for those of his household, he has denied the faith, and is worse than an unbeliever"* (1 Timothy 5:8).

But what if the absent parent is an unbeliever? It makes no difference at all whether he or she is a believer or nonbeliever—the rules are the same. Parents must support their children.

Bottom line: If this means using the law to force parents to meet their responsibilities, so be it. Prior to the mid-1970s it was possible for a parent to avoid paying child support by moving from one state to another. Since local courts had no jurisdiction beyond state boundaries, a warrant for abandonment was not enforceable outside the state. That is no longer true. Federal legislation was passed that makes it possible to extradite a parent for abandonment, including failure to pay child support.

I recommend doing everything possible, outside of filing suit for abandonment. But, all other avenues failing, a parent who refuses to support his or her children should be arrested and jailed if necessary. If the reason for failure to pay is beyond his or her control (illness, unemployment), that obviously should be taken into account. But remember, everybody can pay something, even if it is not everything.

FUTURE INCREASES

It is common for a single mother to take her ex-husband back to court periodically to secure more income for herself or the children.

The issue of "to sue or not to sue" should be clear, from a biblical perspective. If it involves alimony, a spouse should not sue. If it involves child support, the decision must be made on the basis of actual need, not anger or greed. Be certain that all other means of negotiating have been exhausted before appealing to the courts for assistance.

Connie accepted a low child support payment to end a bitter, hostile divorce. Her former spouse worked at construction and suffered layoffs several times during the years she was a single parent. She didn't receive child support at those times, and he never paid the back due amount when he started working again. Because her income was low and didn't meet her expenses, she was counseled repeatedly to take him back to court. But Connie feared his reaction and didn't want to stir up any more trouble, so she decided against it. She figured that if God wanted her to have more, He would have to deal with her former spouse.

To her amazement, the child support didn't stop until three years after their youngest child turned 18, even though her ex-husband was aware that he did not legally have to pay it.

Be certain that your motive is need—not revenge or greed. *"Let your character* [way of life] *be free from the love of money, being content with what you have; for He Himself has said, 'I will never desert you, nor will I ever forsake you'"* (Hebrews 13:5).

A PRACTICAL BUDGET

J ust the mention of the word *budget* arouses negative feelings in some people. They see a budget as something that restricts their fun and freedom. In reality, the exact opposite is true. A budget is merely a plan for how you are going to spend the money you have. It also helps to determine when you have spent all you can without the risk of going into debt.

Many single parents run at the thought of budgeting, even if they are part of the minority that receives adequate child support and makes decent wages. Handling all the financial decisions alone is difficult. Most single parents practice a balancing act to maintain their lifestyles, while paying what comes due and worrying about the rest later. They often feel that their children have gone through so much that they don't want any more disruption in their lives.

So they struggle to keep the family home and provide Christian schooling, extracurricular activities, or private lessons. These expenses often trip them up and prevent them from saving enough to cover emergencies. Many of them resort to credit cards to subsidize their income when emergencies arise, but figuring where to cut back to pay the debt is almost impossible. They believe budgeting would require more time, sacrifice, and discipline than they have to give.

One of the most common statements I hear from single parents is, "I don't really make enough money to budget." What that actually means is, when they balance how much they need to live on against how much they have coming in, the numbers don't come close.

My comment usually is, "Suppose I had someone who wanted to make up your deficit. How would you be able to tell them how much you actually need?"

That usually gets them to thinking. Often the response is, "Well, I think I need about _____ a month to make it."

My next question is, "If you had the funds and were willing to help, would you give to someone who guesses about what he or she needs, or would you give to the person who can demonstrate the need on paper?"

The response is about what you would anticipate. Obviously, if someone were going to help me, that person would expect me to show an actual need. And my benefactor would want to be certain that I would handle the available funds as well as possible. That is all a budget can or should do.

God has promised to meet our needs. But as far as I know, manna is no longer dropped from heaven. In most instances, to help the less fortunate, God uses people to whom He has given a surplus. As God's Word says, *"If a brother or sister is without clothing and in need of daily food, and one of you says to them, 'Go in peace, be warmed and be filled'; and yet you do not give them what is necessary for their body; what use is that?"* (James 2:15-16).

The people who willingly surrender a part of their assets to help others would be poor stewards themselves if they required no accountability from those they help. I personally would not give money to anyone (other than in an emergency) who was not involved in some type of financial counseling and living on a budget. After all, I live on a budget too.

A budget, to be of any value, must be as uncomplicated as possible and still get the job done. When I first began to counsel, I checked out every budget workbook in the stores. I knew I needed something to help the counselees get started, and it had to be simple. If most of them had been able to keep detailed financial records, they probably wouldn't have needed me in the first place. What I discovered was that the budget books available at that time were designed by accountants for accountants—or at least that's the way it seemed.

They were thick books with lots of complicated forms and practically no pictures or examples.

So as I started out to design my own budget workbook, I asked myself, what is the simplest budgeting system available? The answer was deceptively simple—using envelopes to keep your money in.

For instance, if you converted your total income each pay period to cash, divided it into the categories of your spending, and put it into envelopes, you'd have a rudimentary budget. As the payments or expenditures came due, you would draw the money out of the applicable envelope (Housing, Auto, Clothing, Insurance, or one of the others) and pay the bills. Of course, you could always rob one envelope to pay for something you wanted in another category. But then, no budget will control overspending. Only you can do that!

The key to the envelope budget is, when an envelope is empty, you stop spending in that category until the next paycheck.

One more step is necessary if your envelope budget system is to last beyond the next few months: You must anticipate expenses that don't come due every month, such as annual insurance, taxes, car repairs, vacations, gifts, or Christmas gift buying. Then you must allocate these nonmonthly expenditures in other envelopes that will be kept until the expense arises. Most often, it is these little unplanned expenses that will destroy a budget and convince the budgeter that it won't work.

Although I have helped many people develop an envelope budgeting system when I found they could not manage a checking account, I don't recommend it for most people. It's not a good idea to leave that much cash in your home. And learning to maintain a checkbook is not difficult at all—with a little help and a few simple rules.

The budgeting system I have used for many years is based on the envelope system, except that all of the noncurrent spending funds are kept in a checking account. We substitute individual account sheets for the envelopes and a running balance is kept on each category of spending, i.e., Housing, Auto, Food. In other words, all spending decisions are made based on what is in your account sheets—not your checking account. The total balance of all the account sheets will equal what is in the checking account.

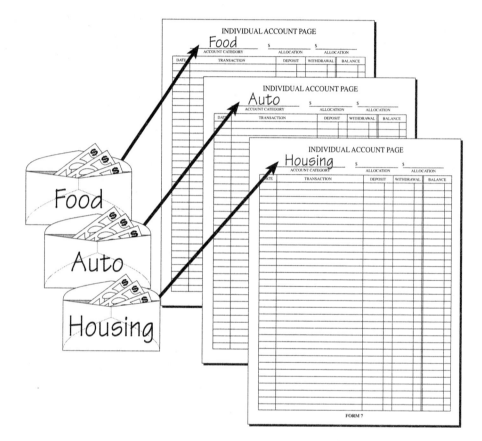

For example, if you need clothes for your child, you don't look to see if there is any money left in the checking account. Instead, you look at the Clothing Allocation Sheet to see if there is any money left in that category. Otherwise, you'll be spending funds that were allocated to another area.

For the categories that cannot be funded because of a lack of money, you have a very specific prayer request. And if the Lord prompts someone to ask about your needs, you will have specific facts to give. I have often seen the Lord bless a good steward who was managing well what he or she had, but that person simply lacked the funds needed for nonmonthly expenses.

In the rest of the chapter I would like to cover a basic budget, category by category, and offer some suggestions on how to budget on a single parent's income. For a broader look at your finances, I would suggest you get the workbook that is a companion to this book. It is *The Financial Guide for the Single Parent.*

The assumption I have made is that you make somewhere near the average income for single parents, so I have used $15,000 per year as a basis for the examples.

The first important principle to know in budgeting is how much Net Spendable Income you have available. Often the percentages that are given for categories like Housing and Auto are based on gross (total) income. This never made any sense to me, since no one actually has their gross income to spend—only net income. So the percentages I will use are after taxes and tithes (assuming that you tithe). This will be called your Net Spendable Income (NSI).

Divide any annual amounts by twelve to arrive at a monthly average.

GROSS INCOME PER MONTH
(totals of 1 through 4 below)   _____
1. Salary, wages, tips, bonuses   _____
   Self-employment income, commissions _____
   Alimony, child support   _____
   Welfare, rent subsidy, Social Security _____
   Disability, V.A., or retirement benefits _____
   Tax refunds   _____
   Total   _____
Note: If your income is irregular, add income
from several low income months and divide
the total by the number of months used.

2. Interest   _____
    Includes checking and savings account interest earned.

3. Dividends   _____
    Includes all money that you receive from investments.

4. Other   _____
    Includes food stamps, regular money gifts—anything
    not added in "income."

SUBTRACT (from Gross Income Per Month)
1. Tithe   _____
    The amount you are currently giving to God's work.

2. Taxes   _____
    Includes federal, state, local, Social Security, FICA,
    self-employment tax.

Note: If you pay self-employment taxes quarterly,
divide the amount by 3 or, if yearly, by twelve
to arrive at the monthly amount.

The results: Net Spendable Income (NSI)   _____

KNOW WHAT YOU SPEND

Once you know how much you have available to budget, the next step is to find out how much you are spending now. You can do this in either of two ways. One, go through your checkbook for the previous year and divide your spending by the categories we will discuss. This presumes you do the majority of your spending out of your checking account, and you don't write one check for multiple categories (such as writing a check for groceries and cash together). Otherwise this method won't work for you. You'll have to go to "plan B."

The second method is to keep a diary for a least one month, which lists everything you buy, category by category. There will be some variable expenses that are not incurred every month, such as car repairs, clothes, vacations, and so on. These must be estimated, based on some average spending estimates.

Let's assume at this point you know how much you have available to spend, and you know (within reason) how much you spend monthly, but the outgo is more than the income. The next step is to look at each category of spending to decide what adjustments can be made.

By looking at each spending category, you can brainstorm ideas to help you budget better. If, after doing all you can to control your spending, you still cannot make your budget balance, you qualify for the help and support of other Christians. If your church does not have an active single parents' benevolence plan, then you need to pray and help get one started.

THE BUDGET CATEGORIES

The percentages on the next page can be used to help you compare current spending to what can be allocated reasonably for each category.

• *Category 1—Taxes.* Everybody has to pay taxes—single parents with inadequate income included. The amount of taxes paid will vary, based on income and expenses, but the one tax virtually no one can escape is Social Security (FICA). If you work for someone else, these taxes are taken out before you are paid. But if you are self-employed through child care services in your home, outside sales of direct marketing products (such as Amway, Mary Kay cosmetics, and so on), or any other sources, you are required to pay Social Security self-employment taxes on income up to approximately $50,000 per year.

Unlike the FICA taken from an employee's pay, which is one-half the total paid in, the entire amount is assessed to the self-employed. There are tax breaks available as of 1990, but that is not a subject of this book. You should contact a good local accountant about any tax questions you might have.

I addressed the subject of taxes here only because in counseling I have often encountered single parents who owed substantial amounts to the IRS because they failed to pay on self-employed income. The direct marketing plans used in home businesses are usually the primary source of self-employment income.

I estimate that the average single parent who makes $15,000 a year will owe less than 10 percent of his or her gross income in all taxes or less, if earned income credit remains available.

PERCENTAGE GUIDE FOR FAMILY INCOME
(Family of Two)

Gross Income	15,000	25,000	35,000	45,000	55,000	65,000
1. Tithe	10%	10%	10%	10%	10%	10%
2. Taxes [1]	13.4%	19.3%	22%	23%	26%	28.5%
NET SPENDABLE INCOME [2]	11,490	17,675	23,800	30,153	35,200	39,975
3. Housing	38%	38%	34%	30%	27%	26%
4. Food	15%	12%	12%	12%	11%	10%
5. Auto	15%	15%	12%	12%	12%	11%
6. Insurance	5%	5%	5%	5%	5%	5%
7. Debts	5%	5%	5%	5%	5%	5%
8. Ent./Recreation	4%	5%	6%	6%	7%	7%
9. Clothing	4%	5%	5%	5%	6%	6%
10. Savings	5%	5%	5%	5%	5%	5%
11. Medical/Dental	5%	5%	4%	4%	4%	4%
12. Miscellaneous	4%	5%	5%	7%	7%	8%
13. Investments [3]	—	—	7%	9%	11%	13%
14. School/Child Care [4]	—	—	—	—	—	—
15. Alimony/Child Support [4]	—	—	—	—	—	—
16. Unalloc. Surplus Inc. [5]	—	—	—	—	—	—

[1] Guideline percentages for tax category include taxes for Social Security, federal, and a small estimated amount for state, based on 1995 rates. At the $15,000 level of income, the Earned Income Credit drastically reduces the tax burden. However, you must have children to qualify.

[2] Begin figuring 100% from your Net Spendable Income, *not* your Gross Income. Categories 3-13 should total 100% of your Net Spendable Income. On this chart, Larry assumes that couples with incomes below $35,000 probably will not be making investments.

[3] This category is used for long-term investment planning, such as college education or retirement.

[4] This category should be used if you marry someone who already has children. If you have this expense, the percentage shown must be deducted from other budget categories.

[5] This category is used when surplus income is received. This would be kept in the checking account to be used within a few weeks; otherwise, it should be transferred to an allocated category.

So remember, you started out with $1,250 a month (based on a $15,000 per year income). You are now down to $1,125.

GROSS INCOME	$15,000/Year	$1,250/Month
LESS TAXES	1,500/Year	125/Month
	$13,500/Year	$1,125/Month

• *Category 2—Tithes.* I have often been asked whether a Christian (who happens to be a single parent) should tithe if the income is already inadequate to meet all the family's needs. Let me summarize what I believe God's Word teaches on this subject. Then let God help you make that decision.

The tithe is meant to be an outside, material indicator that God owns everything in our lives. The first tithe recorded in Scripture was by Abraham in Genesis 14:20, who gave Melchizedek the priest a tenth of all the spoils of battle as a symbol of his gratitude to God for victory. In Hebrews 7:1-9 we are told that Abraham gave this tithe (430 years before the Law came) in order to acknowledge God's ownership over all that he had.

We are told to honor God from the best of our resources. *"Honor the Lord from your wealth, and from the first of all your produce; so your barns will be filled with plenty, and your vats will overflow with new wine"* (Proverbs 3:9-10).

I truly believe that God doesn't need the money, nor is He an accountant checking to see if we're careful to give exactly a tenth. God checks the heart attitude and blesses accordingly. *"Let each one do just as he has purposed in his heart; not grudgingly or under compulsion; for God loves a cheerful giver"* (2 Corinthians 9:7).

Giving, like salvation, is a personal matter between you and God. No one can make you do it; you have a choice. However, the lack of giving is a material indicator that spiritual changes need to be made. Those who give less than a tenth of their increase have limited what God can do for them according to His own Word.

"Will a man rob God? Yet you are robbing Me! But you say, 'How have we robbed Thee?' In tithes and offerings" (Malachi 3:8). God understands your finances better than you do. As your trust in Him grows, so will your giving. Mature Christians give because they love

God and recognize His ownership of everything, including their finances.

For our purposes, I will assume that 10 percent goes to the Lord's work. This leaves you with 80 percent of the original income or $1,000 per month. So that's the total amount that can be spent.

NET INCOME (after taxes)	$13,500/Year	$1,125/Month
LESS TITHE	1,500/Year	125/Month
NET SPENDABLE INCOME (NSI)	**$12,000/Year**	**$1,000/Month**

SPENDING CATEGORIES

All of the following spending categories are allocated out of your NSI. You will notice that the total of all the categories equals 100 percent before child care expenses are deducted. *Therefore, if you have child care expenses, all other categories must be adjusted accordingly.*

If your child support is irregular or your alimony is temporary, allocate the amount to savings or emergency funds. Do not depend on unreliable income for vital expenses like Housing, Auto, or Child Care.

The Financial Guide for the Single Parent Workbook examines each category in detail and offers suggestions for stretching available dollars.

• *Category 3—Housing.* The maximum guideline percentage that can be allocated to housing is approximately 40 percent of NSI *(Net Spendable Income),* or $400 per month. This includes your payments or rent, utilities (including telephone), taxes, maintenance—literally everything associated with housing, including insurance.

Since we have already discussed this topic earlier, I won't spend more time here. The critical factor is to not overspend on housing.

• *Category 4—Food.* This is food that you buy at a grocery store or its equivalent. It does not include eating out or entertaining. Eating out is allocated under entertainment expenses. The maximum percent of NSI that can be allocated to food is approximately 15 percent, or $150 per month. As you must already realize, this is not much money for food for a family of two or three. However, if you elect to spend more in this category, it will have to come out of some other area of your budget.

For most single parents, making the food budget work means shopping discount stores, clipping coupons, hunting specials, buying dented cans, and a myriad of other ideas to reduce costs.

It probably also means that you will need to eliminate most "junk foods," including potato chips, cookies, soft drinks, and the like. It also will mean no prepared foods, such as microwave-ready meals and frozen dinners. The cost of labor in these items is too expensive for most budgets. But take heart. When I grew up these things weren't even thought about yet. Your kids will survive without them, and probably live longer, healthier lives.

• *Category 5—Automobile Expenses.* Your budget can handle approximately 15 percent for all auto-related expenses. This gives you $150 per month for everything, including payments, insurance, maintenance, gas, and replacement.

This is one of the major sources of debt for single parents. Most of them don't have enough income to repair or replace their worn-out cars. And they certainly don't have the income to finance new ones. As noted earlier, this is one of those categories that requires strong self-discipline and trust in God for what you cannot provide for yourself.

Make an absolute commitment that you will not buy a car you can't afford, and you will not use credit cards to buffer your car repair expenses. I have known many people who did and it never gets easier later. Appendix E contains some helpful information on selecting and evaluating the right car for you.

• *Category 6—Insurance.* This includes all insurance not associated with housing or automobile. Your budget can handle approximately 3 percent for this category—just $30 per month. In order to make this category stretch, you must prioritize your insurance needs, the greatest of which is health insurance, while your children are at home. Unless you have access to a group insurance plan at work, the cost of health insurance is beyond the reach of most single parents.

Health Insurance

Alternatives are available if you don't have a company-paid group plan. One is an association of Christians who have banded together to provide a self-insured health plan for those who normally cannot get other coverage. The average monthly cost per family is low. Unfortunately, it may be above this category's allocation of your income; but, to control your health care costs it may be prudent to sacrifice in another area of your budget. Another group functions more like a traditional insurance plan available through associations. The average monthly costs are about the same.

Be sure you thoroughly investigate the plan you're interested in for benefits, deductibles, and exclusions. The following telephone numbers are provided to help with your research: Brotherhood Association, 800-269-4030; Christian Care Ministry, 800-374-2562; All Saints, 800-295-7874; and Good Samaritan, 317-894-2000.

In a real pinch you may want to investigate Medicaid benefits. Many states have adopted rules for Medicaid that make it available to lower income families and any children under age 6. I personally object to any Christians being forced to take government aid. Although I don't see any specific scriptural prohibition against accepting government aid, I do believe it reflects poorly upon the integrity of the other Christians who have a surplus they could share.

As the apostle Paul said, *"At this present time your abundance being a supply for their want, that their abundance also may become a supply for your want, that there may be equality"* (2 Corinthians 8:14).

Life Insurance

Not everyone needs life insurance. However, many single parents worry about having no life insurance in the event of their deaths. This is a valid concern, but with limited dollars life insurance should be a lower priority than health coverage. A questionnaire is provided in Appendix D to help you determine your life insurance needs. If you have determined that you need life insurance and can free even a small amount per month for life insurance, I suggest buying the least expensive type available.

This is normally *annual renewable term* insurance, which means the premiums increase annually. It accumulates no cash values and is normally called "pure insurance." It provides the greatest death benefit for the least current cost. Concern yourself with investments and retirement benefits later. At this point, provision must be your primary concern.

One additional thought on the subject of life insurance is necessary. Many single parents worry about not having any insurance on their children in the event of a child's death. I recommend that you investigate the Memorial Society as a possible alternative. This is a nonprofit group that operates in most states. They help to establish other nonprofit groups, who in turn contract with various funeral homes throughout the nation to provide inexpensive burials. The fee to join is minimal and burial costs average about $500. The costs will vary by state and by area. If you are interested in this program, you can call the Funeral and Memorial Societies of America at 1-800-765-0107.

Other types of insurance, such as disability, are generally too expensive for a single parent to even consider. If you have additional funds to spend, you might investigate this area, but remember that the vast majority of people are not going to become disabled. In the event of total disability, Social Security will provide benefits if you have been in the program at least twenty quarters (five years). Additional information on Social Security benefits is provided in Appendix C. And you can order the free publication from CFC titled "What Every Widow Needs to Know."

• *Category 7—Debts.* In addition to payments on a home or car, the average single parent can handle no more than 4 percent of Net Spendable Income on all debt payments (about $40 per month). "That's fine," you say, "but what happens if I owe $150 a month to creditors?"

In reality you cannot pay that much of your income to creditors and still make your budget balance on an average $15,000 per year income. If you have promised more than a maximum of 10 percent of your net income to creditors, there are three potential solutions (I assume here that a maximum of 10 percent could be worked into the average single parent's budget).

Solution 1. After making out a budget that allows for the normal monthly living expenses, contact each creditor with a plan for how much you can pay them. Never promise more than you can realistically pay. You can always pay more when it *is* possible, but it's very hard to cut back on what's already been promised.

Solution 2. Use an intermediary counselor, such as one of Christian Financial Concepts' volunteer counselors or one available through Consumer Credit Counseling. To request a volunteer counselor, write Christian Financial Concepts, 601 Broad St SE, Gainesville, GA 30501. For more information on Consumer Credit Counseling, check your local phone book or call the national office at 301-589-5600.

Solution 3. File for bankruptcy protection under Chapter 13 of the Federal Bankruptcy Act. This provides court protection while you are attempting to pay back the debts you have incurred. Information on the Federal Bankruptcy Act is available in my book *Debt-Free Living* (Moody Press, 1989).

Any action taken to offset the pressures of creditors must always be weighed against the principles given in God's Word. The first is that God wants His people to honor their commitments: *"It is better that you should not vow than that you should vow and not pay"* (Ecclesiastes 5:5).

The second is that God's people must always repay a legitimate debt. *"The wicked borrows and does not pay back, but the righteous is gracious and gives"* (Psalm 37:21).

I have seen many situations where payment of existing obligations seemed impossible. But once the individuals made the absolute commitment to repay what was legitimately due, God provided the means to do so. I particularly like the promise found in Psalm 50:14-15: *"Offer to God a sacrifice of thanksgiving, and pay your vows to the Most High; and call upon Me in the day of trouble; I shall rescue you, and you will honor Me."*

So you do your part and God will do His part. It won't always be an instantaneous solution, but the old adage is still true: **God is rarely early . . . but never late.**

• *Category 8—Entertainment and Recreation.* Usually when a budget is tight and bills are past due, the first thing to go is all entertainment.

Unfortunately, since no one can really live without occasional recreation, even if it is just eating a hamburger out now and then, the tendency is to spend outside the budget. This usually means the misuse of credit cards and more debt.

A normal single parent's budget, with all the other categories in balance, can allocate about 4 percent of NSI for Entertainment and Recreation. Even those on a tight budget must allocate something each month. I would recommend allocating at least $10 per week—no matter what.

The last thing you want is for your children to look at life as one great sacrifice of all enjoyment. Often they will associate the sacrifice with your faith and assume that to be a Christian means the total abandonment of fun. The best way to combat such a consequence is to be totally honest about your finances and to set aside at least a small amount for this category.

If you're open to God's leading, He can supply your needs even in the area of Entertainment and Recreation. For several years I counseled a single mother with three children, who never had any available funds for being entertained; yet, God always seemed to provide.

One year she was asked by her church to head a youth group summer mission to a sister church in England. Another year she was invited to travel with the seniors group to Europe. Still another she was selected to lead a Bible study during a summer missions building trip to Canada. She was able to take her children on all these trips and share with them the joy of God's miraculous provision. This doesn't mean that God works the same way with everyone. But I do believe that most people never allow God the right to decide such issues.

• *Category 9—Clothing.* About 5 percent of your NSI should be allocated for clothing (about $50 per month for a $15,000 per year income). Two things are apparent at first glance. First, most single parents don't have $50 a month in their budget for clothing. Second, even if they did, $50 won't go very far today for two or three people.

The important thing is to at least allocate something on a monthly basis for replacement of clothing and to eliminate all use of credit cards to buy clothes you cannot afford. Allow God to provide some of your needs from the surpluses of other people. There are many (too many) Christians who have large clothing budgets and, consequently, have clothes in their closets they seldom, if ever, wear.

If you have a clothes closet or benevolence program within your church, many people will make clothes available to those who have a need. But be careful; some people clean out their closets once every ten years and give clothes that are terribly outdated or worn out—things they wouldn't wear themselves. Unfortunately, single parents who've received such offerings are embarrassed and won't let their needs be known.

I remember well the comments of several single parents I have counseled. They said that members of their churches took the position that if they were going to help someone they expected them to look needy. In reality, most of the single parents only bought clothes when they were on sale, in recycled-clothing stores, or in discount stores. Sometimes people in the church had provided them with clothing—especially for their children. Too often the people who reviewed the benevolence fund activities considered these people overdressed.

Let me say further that such an attitude is highly judgmental, petty, and contrary to the Word of God. The apostle Paul says, *"Do nothing from selfishness or empty conceit, but with humility of mind let each of you regard one another as more important than himself"* (Philippians 2:3). The people who judge others in need only by outside appearance are selfish and self-serving.

I have seen many well-dressed single parents who either made their own clothes or shopped outlets, sales, and used clothing stores diligently. These people should be applauded, not criticized. As long as you're not buying at your creditors' expense, don't hesitate to dress as well as you can. Also don't hesitate to share what you've learned with others around you. Some of the best dressed, most affluent people in our churches could use a good dose of conviction themselves.

• *Category 10—Savings.* There are always additional costs in a budget that cannot be anticipated. Therefore some additional savings are needed. I realize that in a budget in which the regular monthly expenses are not being met, a savings account seems like wishful thinking. But until some savings are accumulated for the emergencies, the use of credit cards is a certainty. It is better money management to repair refrigerators and washing machines with your own money rather than with a creditor's.

The allocation for this category should be about 5 percent of NSI. However, if you can't put that much aside, save whatever you can, but make a commitment to start saving something.

One way to do this is to allocate a percentage of all additional income to your budgeted savings. This means irregular child support, temporary alimony, cash gifts, overtime income, bonuses, garage sale profits, and so on. Once you make a commitment to becoming totally debt-free, God can bless you in many ways. But if you never make the commitment, the additional money will likely always be spent. There always seems to be inexhaustible needs in the lives of single parents. Even so, savings must become an absolute priority.

• *Category 11—Medical and Dental Expenses.* The allocation for doctor bills should be at least 5 percent. Unfortunately, this is one of those categories that causes havoc in most single parents' budgets. Even if you are covered by a hospitalization plan through your job, often the deductible and co-pays are beyond your budget. Plus, most companies require the employee to pay part of the premium cost. In addition to the added cost of care, single parents often lose a day or two of work to care for sick children. Many single parents don't have the option to take sick days when their children are sick, and those who do find that sick days add up quickly because their children are exposed to more illnesses through school or day care.

As we discussed earlier, there are no simple solutions to this problem without the help of other people. When your out-of-pocket medical and dental expenses exceed your ability to pay, you must let the other Christians around you know it! There should be no more hesitation to share such financial needs than there would be to share a physical need.

In working with many single parents I have found that some Christian physicians and dentists will provide low- or even no-cost care if they are aware of your circumstances and know you are working with a trained counselor. I would encourage you to be totally honest with them up front. Don't run up large medical bills and then tell them; let the decision to help be theirs.

Sometimes it is possible to work out a barter for much of the health care your family needs. I have known women who cleaned offices, provided tutoring, baby-sitting, and many other exchanges of labor for the medical and dental care their families needed. You really won't know unless you ask.

• *Category 12—Miscellaneous.* This is the category that contains everything that won't fit into any other category. It includes allowances, cash you carry, lunches, cosmetics, haircuts, and the like. The allocation for such expenses is about 4 percent. Unless you diligently control your spending for miscellaneous items, they can consume a great deal of money.

The only way I have ever found to control miscellaneous spending is to allocate only a given amount of money and then stick to it. If you run out before the next pay period, you must learn to do without.

One of the largest expenses within this category is that of gifts, including birthdays, Christmas, and any other celebration. Many single parents (and couples) go deeply into debt for gifts, often because of guilt they feel over the sacrifices of their children. Don't fall into this trap! The short-term gratification of giving gifts won't balance the long-term stress of debt.

Single parents who make a commitment to manage their money correctly must develop some alternatives, such as crafts, to provide the gifts they need. Children won't feel deprived because of less gift giving. It's only because of our indulgence-crazy society that children (and parents) have the unrealistic expectations they do today. We can all stand to do some soul searching about the indulgent gifts we think children "need."

For several years when our children were small we made crafts for gifts. I can honestly say that I don't have one single gift my children ever bought me, but I still have several of those they made for me. We live in a generation with a warped sense of values. Teach your children that it takes more love to make gifts than it does to buy them.

• *Category 13—Child Care/School/Child Support.* The normal family budget allocation for this category is 8 to 15 percent of NSI. If you have been adding up the various categories, you will note that there are no percentages remaining for child care. This is because it is not a normal expenditure for many single parents. About 40 percent of single parents have to face the financial burden of daily child care. The others either work in the home, don't work a full-time job, or have parents who help.

For those who do pay for child care, private school, or child support, 8 to 15 percent is about all they can work into their budgets realistically. There's no magical formula to making these expenses fit into your budget. It's a matter of taking the necessary funds out of the other categories. When looking at 100 percent of spending it looks simple enough to subtract 8 to 15 percent for child care expenses, until you get down to which category to reduce. Then you may well decide that it's impossible. But it has to be done if your budget is ever to balance.

What are the logical categories to reduce? As difficult as it is, the *Housing* category can be reduced by 5 percent or so. In some areas of the country it's relatively simple. In other areas there is no way to reduce single family housing costs to $350 a month. Virtually the only option is to look for someone you can share housing costs with.

Food, Auto, Clothing, Savings, Entertainment, and *Insurance* can all be reduced by 1 percent to free the additional funds needed. These are usually the categories that get slashed to provide needed funds. It's not easy, but it is better to reduce these categories by about 1 percent each, to free the additional funds needed, instead of cutting them drastically or eliminating them entirely.

Before reducing other areas, check to see if any individuals or churches in your area provide child care on a sliding scale fee according to income, especially if you have preschool age children.

STEPS IN BUDGETING

You will find an outline for beginning a budget in Appendix A of this book. This information is covered in more detail in *The Financial Guide for the Single Parent* workbook, which includes original, full-size copies of the forms used. The workbook should be available in your local Christian bookstore, or you can order direct from Christian Financial Concepts.

LONG-RANGE PLANNING

There are two questions often asked by single parents: "How will I ever be able to send my child to college?" and "What will I be able to do about retirement?"

There are no simple answers to these questions, except for what the Lord said. *"Therefore do not be anxious for tomorrow; for tomorrow will care for itself. Each day has enough trouble of its own"* (Matthew 6:34). If you commit yourself to becoming the best steward you can be right now, that's the best you can do.

If God wants your children to have a college education, He can and will provide. The same is true of retirement. You don't want to be slothful and ignore the future, but you are only responsible to do what you can do—not what you cannot do.

As soon as your children are old enough to begin earning their own money, start them on a budget of their own, with a portion of all they earn set aside for long-term goals, such as education. They can earn a substantial portion of what they will need later if you will help them get started early enough. After all, only a generation ago that was the normal way to go to college.

A small amount saved regularly can amount to a great deal of money. For instance, assume your child started saving $10 a month at age 10, increased that to $20 a month at age 13, then to $30 a month from age 15 until college age (18). Assuming it was invested in U.S. Series E bonds and used for college so the earnings would be tax free, they would have nearly $3,000 available. Clearly, that's not all they will need, but it's a good start.

Appendix A

STEPS TO MAKING A BUDGET

The following material is provided as a practical guide to help you establish a budget. It is not a detailed instruction on budgeting. For more information, ask your local bookstore for a copy of *The Financial Guide for the Single Parent* workbook.

STEPS TO MAKING A BUDGET

In making and using a budget, there are several logical steps, each requiring individual effort. A sample form for budgeting is shown in Figure B, page 187. Use this form to guide your budget preparation.

STEP 1—COMPARE

a. If you haven't assessed your current spending levels (in Chapter 10), do that now, using Figure B, page 187. This form will guide your budget preparation.

(1) Fill in your Gross Income, Tithe, and Taxes to get your Net Spendable Income.
(2) Fill in your fixed expenses, for example:
   mortgage payments or rent
   garbage pickup
   telephone
   home or renter's insurance

> child care (if same amount is paid every month, summer included)
> auto loan payment, auto insurance, gas

(3) Now include all variable expenses:
> food
> outstanding debts
> utilities
> insurance (life, health)
> clothing
> medical/dental
> savings
> entertainment/recreation (includes eating out)
> miscellaneous

b. Use the percentage guidelines on page 168 to compare present spending to recommended spending for each category. Don't be concerned at this point if you do not have money allocated for all the budgeting categories. Many single parents don't. Start where you are.

STEP 2—ANALYZE

a. If you have a deficit:
   (1) Determine where you are overspending.
   (2) Determine where you can make cuts to provide funds for necessary categories.

STEP 3—DECIDE

a. If total income exceeds total expenses, you only have to implement a method of budget control in your home. However, if expenses exceed income (or more stringent controls in spending are desired), additional steps are necessary. In that case, an analysis of each budget area is called for to reduce expenses. The following will help you to establish your new budget.

b. If necessary funds cannot be extracted from your current spending:
   (1) Decide what changes in lifestyle can be made. (See the single parent workbook for ideas that have worked for other single parents.)

(2) Seek the help of a financial advisor, such as one of CFC's volunteer counselors or someone from Consumer Credit Counseling.

(3) Seek the help of other Christians.

BUDGET PROBLEM AREAS

Bookkeeping Errors

An accurately balanced checkbook is a must. Even small errors result in big problems if they are allowed to compound.

An inaccurate balance can result in an overdrawn account, as well as in significant bank charges.

Automatic banking systems create additional pitfalls. Automatic payment deductions must be subtracted from the checkbook ledger at the time they are paid by the bank.

For example, an insurance premium is paid by automatic withdrawal on the fifteenth of each month. Since no statement or notice is received from the insurance company, you must be certain that on the fifteenth of every month the proper amount is deducted from your home checking account records. The same would be true for automatic credit card payments or any other automatic withdrawal.

Direct deposits into checking accounts must also be noted in the home ledger at the proper time. Don't forget to include bank service charges in the home ledger.

If you withdraw cash from your account using an automatic teller machine, be sure you write it in your ledger and file the transaction record.

FACTORS IN KEEPING GOOD RECORDS

1. Use a ledger type checkbook rather than a stub type. The ledger gives greater visibility and lends itself to fewer errors. I usually recommend using a checkbook that has a duplicate copy of the checks written. This eliminates errors in not posting a check.

2. Be certain all checks are accounted for. All checks should be entered in the ledger when written. This entry must include the check number, amount, date, and assignee.

Tearing checks out of your checkbook for future use defeats many of the safeguards built into this system. I recommend that all checks be written from the checkbook only.

3. Maintain a home ledger. If all records are kept in a checkbook ledger you run the risk of losing it. A home ledger eliminates this possibility and makes record keeping more orderly. Figure A is an example of a typical checkbook ledger form.

CHECKBOOK LEDGER						
DATE	CK. #	TRANSACTION		DEPOSIT	WITHDRAWAL	BALANCE
12/1		Deposit	○	$755 00		$755 00
12/5	1105	First Finance Co.	③		$423 00	332 00
12/5	1106	Sam's Supermarket	④		60 00	272 00
12/9	1107	GMAC - Payment	⑤			
12/15		Deposit	○			410 00
12/20	1108	Sam's Supermarket	○		130 00	280 00
12/20	1109	City Taxes	○		40 00	240 00
			○		70 00	170 00
12/30		Service Charge	⑫		8 00	162 00
			○			
			○			
			○			
			○			

FIGURE A

USE OF THE CHECKBOOK LEDGER

Note that in the checkbook ledger each deposit and withdrawal is recorded, and the outstanding balance is shown. At the end of each month the ledger is balanced against the bank statement. Also, the total balance in the ledger is then compared to the balance on the budget's Individual Account Sheets.

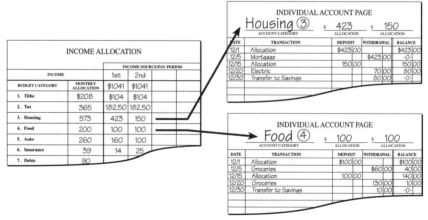

Balance in checking must equal combined balances on account sheets.

INDIVIDUAL ACCOUNT PAGE

Housing ③ $ 423 $ 150
ACCOUNT CATEGORY   ALLOCATION   ALLOCATION

DATE	TRANSACTION	DEPOSIT	WITHDRAWAL	BALANCE
12/1	Allocation	$423 00		$423 00
12/5	Mortgage		$423 00	-0-
12/15	Allocation	150 00		150 00
12/20	Electric		70 00	80 00
12/30	Transfer to Savings		80 00	-0-

SAVINGS ACCOUNT ALLOCATIONS

Date	Deposit	With-drawal	Balance	Housing	Food	Auto Insur.	Auto Maint.	Insur-ance	Clothes	Medical			
12/30	$170		$170	$80	$10		$80						

If there are additional deposits or withdrawals from the bank statement recorded in the Checkbook Ledger, these also must be posted in the appropriate individual account form. For example, a service charge from the bank would be posted as an expense in the Checkbook Ledger and as a miscellaneous expense in category 12 of the budget.

CHECKBOOK LEDGER

DATE	CK. #	TRANSACTION		DEPOSIT	WITHDRAWAL	BALANCE
12/1		Deposit	○	$755 00		$755 00
12/5	1105	First Finance Co.	③		$423 00	332 00
12/5	1106	Sam's Supermarket	④		60 00	272 00
12/9	1107	GMAC - Payment	⑤			
12/15		Deposit	○			410 00
12/20	1108	Sam's Supermarket	○		130 00	280 00
12/20	1109	City Taxes	○		40 00	240 00
			○		70 00	170 00
12/30		Service Charge	⑫		8 00	162 00
			○			
			○			
			○			
			○			

INDIVIDUAL ACCOUNT PAGE

Miscellaneous ⑫ $ 38 $ 38
ACCOUNT CATEGORY   ALLOCATION   ALLOCATION

DATE	TRANSACTION	DEPOSIT	WITHDRAWAL	BALANCE
12/1	Allocation	$38 00		$38 00
12/15	Allocation	38 00		76 00
12/30	Service Charge		$8 00	68 00
12/30	Transfer to Savings		68 00	-0-

Note that the circle (o) on the Checkbook Ledger is used to indicate the category to which the check has been allocated in the budget. This is filled in only after the check has been recorded in the proper budget category.

185

ACCOUNTING—ALLOCATION—CONTROL

A budget that is not used is a waste of time and effort. The most common reason a budget is discarded is because it's too complicated.

The system described in this book is the simplest, yet most complete possible.

Keep It Simple

The Goal—Establish a level of spending for each category so that more money in does not mean more money to spend; and, know where you are with respect to that level at all times.

This budget system is comparable to the old envelope system. In the past, many employers paid earnings in cash. To control spending, families established an effective system by dividing the available money into the various budget categories (Housing, Food, Clothes, and so on)—then holding it in individual envelopes.

As a need or payment came due, money was withdrawn from the appropriate envelope and spent.

The system was simple and, when used properly, quite effective for controlling spending. The rule was simple: When an envelope was empty, there was no more spending for that category. Money could be taken from another envelope, but a decision had to be made—immediately.

Since most families today get paid by check, and since holding cash in the home is not always advisable, a different cash allocation system is necessary.

It is important to know how much should be spent, how much is being spent, and how much is left to spend in each budget category. To accomplish this, account control pages have been substituted for envelopes. All the money is deposited into a checking account and individual account forms are used to accomplish what the envelopes once accomplished. How much is put into each account (or envelope) from monies received during the month is determined from the Monthly Income & Expenses sheet (Figure B).

MONTHLY INCOME & EXPENSES

GROSS INCOME PER MONTH _____

  Salary _____
  Interest _____
  Dividends _____
  Other _____

LESS:

1. Tithe _____

2. Tax (Est. - Incl. Fed., State, FICA) _____

NET SPENDABLE INCOME _____

3. Housing _____
  Mortgage (rent) _____
  Insurance _____
  Taxes _____
  Electricity _____
  Gas _____
  Water _____
  Sanitation _____
  Telephone _____
  Maintenance _____
  Other _____

4. Food _____

5. Automobile(s) _____
  Payments _____
  Gas & Oil _____
  Insurance _____
  License/Taxes _____
  Maint./Repair/Replace _____

6. Insurance _____
  Life _____
  Medical \ _____
  Other _____

7. Debts _____
  Credit Card _____
  Loans & Notes _____
  Other _____

8. Enter. & Recreation _____
  Eating Out _____
  Baby Sitters _____
  Activities/Trips _____
  Vacation _____
  Other _____

9. Clothing _____

10. Savings _____

11. Medical Expenses _____
  Doctor _____
  Dentist _____
  Drugs _____
  Other _____

12. Miscellaneous _____
  Toiletry, cosmetics _____
  Beauty, barber _____
  Laundry, cleaning _____
  Allowances, lunches _____
  Subscriptions _____
  Gifts (incl. Christmas) _____
  Cash _____
  Other _____

13. School/Child Care _____
  Tuition _____
  Materials _____
  Transportation _____
  Day Care _____

14. Investments _____

TOTAL EXPENSES _____

INCOME VS. EXPENSES
  Net Spendable Income _____
  Less Expenses _____
_____

15. Unallocated Surplus Income [1] _____

[1] This category is used when extra unbudgeted money is received, which would be kept in the checking account to be used within a few weeks; otherwise, it should be transferred to a budgeted category.

FORM 1

FIGURE B

187

INCOME ALLOCATION

		INCOME SOURCE/PAY PERIOD			
INCOME					
BUDGET CATEGORY	**MONTHLY ALLOCATION**				
1. Tithe					
2. Tax					
3. Housing					
4. Food					
5. Auto					
6. Insurance					
7. Debts					
8. Entertainment & Recreation					
9. Clothing					
10. Savings					
11. Medical/Dental					
12. Miscellaneous					
13. School/Child Care					
14. Investments					
15. Unallocated Surplus Income					

FIGURE C

HOW TO USE THE BUDGET SYSTEM

A good budget system should be kept as simple as possible while still accomplishing its goal: to tell you if you spend more than you allocated each month. Remember that this system is similar to using envelopes. If a specific amount of money is placed in the envelopes each month, you will know at a glance whether or not your budget balances. Obviously, with some nonmonthly expenses to be budgeted, the ledger system has to be a little more complicated, but don't overcomplicate it.

To help you better understand how to use the budget system, we will take one category (Housing) through a typical month's transactions (see example here and page _____).

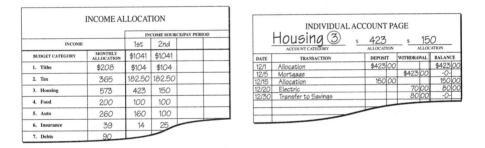

FIGURE D

This illustration shows a budget in which the gross income of $2,082 per month is received in two pay periods of $1,041 each.

Pay Allocation—The two checks have been divided as evenly as possible among the necessary categories. For example, the tithe is paid each pay period (remember, it is based on gross income). The Housing allocation of $573 is divided: $423 in the first pay period, $150 in the second.

Housing Allocation—On the first pay period, a deposit of $423 is noted on the account page. On the fifth of the month, the mortgage is paid and noted as a withdrawal, leaving a zero balance.

Each transaction is noted similarly until, at the end of the month, a balance of $80 is left. This balance is then transferred to savings, as are month-end balances from the other account pages (Food, Savings, and so forth). Hence, each account starts at zero the next month.

Many people prefer to leave the surplus funds from each category in their checking account, rather than transfer them to a savings account. This is fine, if you can discipline yourself not to spend the money just because it's easily accessible. Often the total cash reserves in checking are enough to qualify for free checking privileges, which more than offset any loss of interest in a savings account.

NOTE: In many cases, the housing account may have to carry a surplus forward to make the mortgage payment if it comes due on the first of the month.

POTENTIAL PROBLEM AREAS

Cash Withdrawals—Many times miscellaneous expenditures are made with personal cash. In establishing a budget, it is important to develop some rules for self-discipline.

1. Separate personal cash into categories identical to the account pages. Use envelopes if necessary, but avoid spending gas money for lunches and grocery money for entertainment.
2. When all the money has been spent from a category (Clothing, Entertainment, Miscellaneous), stop spending!
3. Don't write checks for amounts in excess of actual purchases to get cash. Write another check and note it as "cash, personal."

Category Mixing—Don't try to make the record-keeping more complicated than necessary. This system should require no more than thirty minutes per week to maintain. If you choose to develop more detailed breakdowns of expenses and savings, wait until the budget has been in use at least six months.

AUTOMATIC OVERDRAFTS

Many banks offer an automatic overdraft protection service. Thus, if you write a check in excess of what you have in your account, the bank will still honor it. On the surface this looks like a helpful service. However, it has been my experience that overdraft protection tends to create a complacent attitude about balancing the account and encourages overdrafting. Since these charges are accrued to a credit account, you will end up paying interest on your overdrafts. Avoid overdraft protection until your budgeting routine is well established. Perhaps by then it will be unnecessary.

BUDGETING ON A VARIABLE INCOME

One of the most difficult problems in budgeting is how to allocate monthly spending when your income fluctuates, as it often does on commission sales. The normal tendency is to spend the money as it comes in. This works great during the high income months but usually causes havoc during the lower income months.

Two suggestions will help anyone living on a fluctuating income: First, always separate any business-related expenses, such as car maintenance, meals, living accommodations, and the like, from your normal household expenses. I recommend a separate checking account for business expenses and separate credit cards, if needed.

Second, you need to estimate what your (low) average income for one year will be and generate your monthly budget based on the "average" income per month. As the funds come in, they need to be deposited in a special savings account and a salary drawn from the account. The effect is to ration the income over the year in relatively equal amounts that can be budgeted.

Remember, if you are self-employed you will need to budget for payroll taxes on a quarterly basis. Failure to do this will result in a rather unpleasant visit with representatives of the Internal Revenue Service.

If you are beginning your budget during one of the lower income months, you may have to delay funding some of the variable expenses, such as Clothing, Entertainment, Medical, and the like. These can be funded later when the income allows.

WHAT IF YOU ARE PAID EVERY TWO WEEKS?

If you are paid every two weeks rather than twice monthly, you will have two extra paychecks a year. I recommend using these paychecks to fund some of the nonmonthly expenses, such as car repairs, vacations, gifts, and the like. The same would be true of irregular child support, tax refunds, bonuses, and gifts.

Appendix B

WILLS AND TRUSTS

The vast majority of Americans do not have a will or a trust. If they died today they would leave the distribution of their assets to the state. This represents poor stewardship. Most people recognize the need to have a will, but they never get around to (or think they can't afford to) have one drawn. Many others had a valid will at one time, but either circumstances or state laws changed, invalidating their wills.

Regardless of the reason, the simple truth is that if your will cannot be probated (proved) in court, it is worthless. In most states the effect is swift and certain. The state agency assigned to handle intestate (having no legal will) properties will divide them among the surviving heirs (after extracting probate costs, state inheritance taxes, and federal inheritance taxes).

Rather than spend a few hundred dollars in attorney costs, many of these estates will spend several times that in court costs before the assets are distributed. A simple will can avoid these problems. For more complicated estates, consisting of larger assets, a trust may be more advantageous.

Perhaps the best way to discuss this issue is in a question-and-answer format. This will help you to understand what kind of estate planning is best for your family.

1. Can I draft my own will or trust without having to pay an attorney?

Yes, you can in the majority of states. A self-drawn will is called a *holographic* will, which means it is written totally in the handwriting of the person drafting it. The rules governing holographic wills vary from state to state, and to ensure that it is provable in court, your will must adhere to the laws of your state.

Although there are guides available through CFC and in most bookstores for drafting your own will or trust, I would not recommend it. Any flaw in the will can invalidate the entire document. If you do it wrong, it's too late to correct it after you die. It's just not worth the risk for any potentially taxable estate.

Will kits are better used to help you gather the documents and information you need before contacting an attorney. To locate a Christian attorney who specializes in probate and estate planning in your area, call the Christian Legal Society at 703-642-1070.

2. What is probate?

The term *probate* means to prove or to testify. Probate takes place in the probate court of the county in which you reside. It is a legal proceeding to determine the extent of your assets, their value, and how they will be distributed after you die. It is necessary to protect your assets for your heirs creditors, and other persons you owe from the estate and to ensure the collection of money due the estate. Probate provides payment for outstanding debts, taxes, and administration and distribution of the estate; then the remainder goes to the heirs. This process requires considerable paperwork, and it is not uncommon for the legal process to take one or more years.

3. Who handles the administration of my estate?

You can name anyone you want to act as *executor* of your will and estate. Choosing a competent and worthy executor is very important. You should always name at least three alternatives, in the event the executor cannot or will not serve. The executor may or may not receive compensation from the estate. If you have chosen a professional executor, there will be a fee involved, which can vary from an hourly fee to a percentage of the estate value. Any such fees should be clearly stated in a contract and attached to the will.

4. *What are the executor's responsibilities?*

That person's duties may include reading the will to the heirs, distributing property or funds, selling assets, paying debts and taxes, and any other functions specified in the will. The administrator carries out the instructions of the probate judge.

5. *What if one of my witnesses has died?*

Check with a knowledgeable attorney for the requirements in your state. Even if your state requires a minimum of two witnesses, you may not need to choose another one.

6. *What if I change my mind after I make a will?*

You can change your will through the use of a *codicil* (supplement). The codicil is subject to the same laws of probate as the will, so it is important that it be drafted properly. Attach all codicils to the original will and store them together. Remember that only the original will or codicil is probatable, so protect the documents carefully. If you have previous wills in existence, you should specify that your latest will supersedes all previous wills so the judge won't think you are simply adding to an existing document.

7. *Where should I keep my will?*

The original copy of your will should be kept in a safe location because only the original will can be probated. I suggest keeping it at your accountant's or attorney's office, with a note in your home files where it is located. Keeping it in a safe deposit box is not recommended because, unless someone has a key and is authorized to enter your safe deposit box, it could take a court order to open it after your death and could delay probate for months. If no one knows about the box, it might be impossible to locate the original will.

8. *Do I need a new will if I move to another state?*

Possibly. You need to have an attorney in the new state review your will to ensure that it conforms to the new state's laws.

9. What if I own property in more than one state?

Generally, your estate is governed by the state in which you live at the time of your death. A valid will drawn in one state may not control the distribution of assets in another state because that state's laws may be different. Thus the will would need to be probated in each state in which you own property. You should clearly identify all properties in a statement attached to your will, and you will need to pay any taxes due in each state.

10. What is a trust?

A *trust* is a legal contract to manage your assets before and after death. There are two types of trusts: *inter vivos* trust, also known as a "living" trust, which is drafted and implemented while you are still living; and a *testamentary* trust, which commences upon your death.

Trusts may be *revocable* or *irrevocable*. If it is revocable, you reserve the right to modify or cancel the trust and remove or substitute property while you are alive. An irrevocable trust means that it cannot be changed once in force; nor can you recover the property assigned to it.

11. What is the advantage of a living trust?

Living trusts are becoming more popular. Since it is not a public document, it does not require probate and ensures greater privacy. Also, there are no probate costs associated with assets held in a living trust. Since a testamentary trust is normally created within a will, the will must first be probated *before* the trust becomes effective and, consequently, does not avoid probate costs on assets. An attorney can evaluate the assets and liabilities of trusts.

12. How do I choose a trustee?

Unlike the duties of an executor, which are over once the terms of the will are satisfied, the trustee's duties are much longer term. A trust document is normally meant to handle and disperse assets for a long period of time and requires periodic accounting and tax reporting. Thus, naming a trustee is somewhat more complicated and should be done after careful evaluation of the skills and experience necessary. The trustee can be empowered to buy or sell for the estate and transact any business necessary in the name of the trust. The power of the trustee is stated in the trust document.

Cotrustees can be named, and successors should always be specified. As in the case of an executor, a professional trustee always should be named, in the event no other named trustee is able to serve.

13. How much tax will my estate have to pay?

That depends on the value of your estate at death. Your attorney should be able to advise you about potential taxes against your estate. There are two types of taxes: *federal estate taxes* and *state death taxes*. Poor planning can result in some significant federal estate taxes. Surviving children could receive less than 50 percent of the estate through taxes. In fact, the greatest potential tax liability usually involves estates where there is no surviving spouse.

If you remarry, your surviving spouse can receive an unlimited amount of assets through inheritance without incurring any federal estate taxes. Any other beneficiaries can receive up to $600,000 in assets without incurring federal estate taxes. This is a cumulative total of all assets distributed to all the beneficiaries. Above this amount the estate is subject to a progressive federal estate tax. You may think you would never have that much to leave, but you could by the time you include all insurance policies, your home, possessions, car, and any other investments.

Up to $10,000 per year per donor ($20,000 for a couple) may be given to heirs before your death to reduce taxes. The gift taxes paid in the year of transfer represent a credit against potential estate taxes.

Good estate planning is essential for any estate with assets exceeding $600,000. Otherwise the assets can be severely diluted through estate and death taxes when you die. It would be far better stewardship to leave those assets to the Lord's work than to donate them involuntarily to the government.

Many states have adopted the same code for death taxes as the federal government, but several have not. If you happen to live in one of the states that tax an inheritance, the financial shock for survivors can be severe. Many people have actually changed states of primary residence just for this reason.

State death taxes can change as time passes. If you have a question about the taxes in your state, contact your state tax commissioner's office and ask for a current tax table. Remember that state death taxes are graduated and, as such, will increase as the estate grows. This is particularly important for single parents leaving assets to their children. A trust can help reduce estate taxes.

14. When are the taxes due?

If a federal tax return needs to be filed for your estate, the return is due nine months from the date of your death. Therefore, it is imperative for an attorney to be involved in settling your estate immediately so that he or she will have adequate time to prepare the necessary tax returns. Liquidity (cash) in an estate is very important since the taxes must be paid in cash. However, both the state and federal tax collectors will normally work out a plan to convert the assets necessary to pay the taxes so the estate doesn't suffer a severe dilution through a forced sale.

15. What is a charitable trust?

Charitable trusts are increasingly popular among Christians. These trusts are often called *charitable remainder trusts* because the residual in the trust must go to a qualified charitable organization upon the death of the donor.

The donor reserves a lifetime income from the assets assigned to the trust, which is usually managed by the charitable beneficiary. Because a portion of the assets will eventually go to the charity (one or more), the donor is allowed a current charitable deduction from income taxes at the time of assignment to the trust. This amount is calculated by the IRS on the basis of how much benefit the donor receives during his or her lifetime, versus how much the charity will eventually receive.

Obviously, the assets remaining in the trust at the time of the donor's death are not subject to taxation.

16. Are gift annuities the same as charitable trusts?

A *gift annuity* works much the same as a charitable remainder trust in that the donor assigns assets (usually cash or marketable securities) in exchange for a lifetime income, or annuity. The donor is allowed a current charitable deduction on his or her income taxes based on the remainder value that the charity will receive.

The primary difference between the charitable remainder trust and the gift annuity is that the donor is guaranteed the income from a charitable remainder trust only as long as there are available assets earning income. If the assets are depleted, the income stops.

In a gift annuity the income is guaranteed for as long as the donor lives, regardless of whether the assets are depleted. Usually the percentages of guaranteed income from a gift annuity will be less than that from a charitable trust. The logic of this is obvious: contingent liability on the part of the charity.

If you want more information or want to designate CFC in charitable trust, call the main office number at 770-534-1000 and ask for the planned giving department, or call an estate planner in your area.

SOCIAL SECURITY AND VETERANS' BENEFITS

SOCIAL SECURITY BENEFITS

Most people are aware that Social Security offers retirement benefits. To qualify for benefits you must be at least 62 years old and be fully insured. A person employed for at least ten years in jobs covered by Social Security normally can assume to be fully vested (insured), which means that he or she will receive full benefits. Fewer quarters of participation or lower pay-in will reduce the amount of the benefits paid.

However, many single parents don't realize that they or their children may be eligible to receive survivor's benefits if a spouse dies. Benefits depend upon certain criteria, such as how long you were married, if you are remarried at the time of death, and the age and dependency status of the child. A parent can receive benefit payments based on taking care of that child until he or she reaches age 16 (unless the child is disabled). Plus, a child can receive benefit payments in his or her own right until age 18 if that child is a full-time student.

To help with burial expenses, Social Security pays a one-time $255 lump sum to the children of insured members. To receive this benefit a proof of death (death certificate) must be shown.

If you have never requested an evaluation of benefits you've accumulated from Social Security, I would suggest doing so as soon as possible. Even though there is no longer a statute of limitations for making corrections to your account, the sooner any errors are discovered, the easier the correction process will be. Contact the Social Security Administration in your community or call 1-800-234-5772 to request the proper forms.

DISABILITY BENEFITS

A fully insured participant may qualify for disability benefits. Unlike survivor's or retirement benefits, disability payments are not dependent on the age of the recipients but on the proof of disability. Meeting the requirements for disability benefits is not easy, but there are exceptions for persons disabled before reaching age 31 and for the blind. To qualify as disabled you must meet *all* of the following conditions.

- Be under the age of 65 and have enough Social Security coverage when the waiting period of disability benefits begins. At present there is a five-month waiting period, and payments start in the sixth full month of disability.
- The degree of your disability must be severe enough to prevent you from doing any substantial, gainful work.
- The disability must last (or be expected to last) for at least twelve months or result in death.
- You must have accumulated at least twenty quarters of coverage under the system in the forty-quarter period that ends in the quarter you became disabled.

Disability benefits also may be paid to disabled children past the age of 22 if they were disabled before reaching age 22 and have remained disabled. Persons entitled to disability benefits for twenty-four successive months also qualify for Medicare benefits.

VETERAN'S BENEFITS

If a child under 18 years of age has a parent who is a veteran, that child may qualify for veteran's benefits in the event of the veteran's death.

Generally, to qualify for V.A. benefits, a veteran's active duty service must have been terminated under honorable conditions. Even though an honorable or general discharge will qualify a veteran for most benefits, a dishonorable discharge usually disqualifies a veteran for most benefits. A bad conduct discharge may enable the veteran to qualify for some benefits, depending on the V.A.'s determination of facts surrounding the member's discharge.

Education Benefits

If a veteran dies or is permanently and totally disabled as a result of military service, his or her minor children may qualify to receive financial help for educational purposes.

Instruction can be in an approved vocational school, business school, college, professional school, or a business having an apprentice or on-the-job training program. It also includes instruction in a secondary school, by correspondence, or in an educational institution offering farm co-op programs.

Normally, the length of schooling cannot exceed forty-five months of full-time courses, or the equivalent of forty-five months, if enrolled on a part-time basis. A child's marital status is not a barrier to receiving these benefits.

Dependency and Indemnity Benefits

The payment of Dependency and Indemnity Compensation (DIC) was originally intended to assist the surviving spouse and dependent children of a veteran whose death resulted from a service-connected disability or cause. Changes in the law have broadened the scope of DIC benefits to include the survivors of certain veterans whose deaths do not meet the earlier (and more stringent) rules.

When Death Is Due to a Non-Service-Connected Cause

DIC payments can be authorized to certain survivors of veterans who were totally disabled from a service-connected cause, but whose deaths were not the result of that service-connected cause or disability. Benefits are payable if the veteran was

(1) Continuously rated as totally disabled for a period of ten (10) years or more; or

(2) If so rated for less than ten (10) years, was so rated for at least five years from the date he or she was discharged.

Benefit payments are authorized for the veteran's unmarried children under the age of 18 (under 23 if they're students) and to certain helpless children.

Death Pension

Based on financial need and ability to qualify, a veteran's surviving unmarried children under 18 (under 23 if students) may be entitled to a monthly V.A. pension.

For the survivors to qualify, the deceased veteran must have had at least ninety (90) days of service and must have been separated or discharged under conditions other than dishonorable—unless the separation was due to a service-connected disability. If the veteran died while serving on active duty, but the death was not in the line of duty, benefits may be payable if he or she had completed at least two years of honorable active military service.

V.A. Burial Benefit

Veterans Affairs will furnish a headstone or marker to memorialize or mark the grave of a veteran buried in a national, state, or private cemetery. The V.A. also provides markers to eligible family members interred in a national or state veterans' cemetery.

If death is not service-connected, the V.A. provides a burial allowance of $300, if the veteran was entitled at the time of death to V.A. compensation or died in a V.A. medical facility. A plot or interment allowance of $150 is also available if the veteran is entitled to the burial allowance, served during a war period, or was discharged or retired from service because of a disability that was incurred or aggravated in the line of duty. A veteran buried in a national or other federal cemetery, however, is not eligible for this plot allowance. The plot allowance may be paid to a state if the veteran was buried in a state veterans' cemetery.

If the death is service-connected, the V.A. will pay an amount not to exceed $1,000 in lieu of the burial and plot allowance. The V.A. also will provide an American flag for use in covering a casket; a reimbursement is likewise available for part of the cost of a private headstone or marker bought after the veteran's death. (The current amount is $71.)

For further information, contact Veteran's Affairs, 810 Vermont Ave NW, Washington, DC 20420.

Appendix D

INSURANCE BENEFITS

The minimum amount of life insurance you should have is an amount sufficient to provide the needs during an adjustment period for your minor children and any ongoing care they may need in the event of your death. If your children's other parent or other family members are available and able to care for them, the amount you need could be much lower.

Paying off your mortgage and debts also will reduce the amount needed. However, putting your money into current needs, or saving it in higher earning investments for lump sum expenses like education, would be a better use of your current income than buying insurance.

Copy the Insurance Needs worksheet on page 206 to figure your insurance needs. If you discover that a large amount would be needed and funds are limited, renewable term insurance would provide the most coverage for the lowest initial cost.

INSURANCE NEEDS
WORKSHEET FOR SINGLE PARENTS

There are certain expenses you need to plan for in the event that you die prematurely, especially if you are the sole provider for your minor children. To figure your insurance needs, fill out any of the following that applies to you.

If any figures represent a monthly or yearly amount, multiply monthly amounts by twelve for a yearly amount, and multiply yearly amounts by the number of years the children would need the provision for a total amount in each category.

Example:

Child care $400 per month x 12 = $4,800 per year

If child care would be needed for 3 years:

$4,800 x 3 = $14,400 (total amount)

1. Available Income

Since your income would be lost, consider other sources of income. Would the other parent care for the children or provide support? Are there any benefits that your children would be eligible to receive if you died?

Income from other parent_____ x _____ = _____
                                Per year   Number of years   Total amount

Social Security benefits   _____ x _____ = _____
                                Per year   Number of years   Total amount

Veteran's benefits   _____ x _____ = _____
                                Per year   Number of years   Total amount

Other   _____ x _____ = _____
                                Per year   Number of years   Total amount

Total available income (add all totals in section 1)   _____
                                                         Total amount

206

2. *Additional Income Needed*

Lump sums may be required for specific purposes. For example, how much will you need to provide for your children's college educations? If your children are college age now, how much would you need to contribute to complete their educations? If your children will be expected to help pay for college, if financial aid will be available, or if their other parent will help pay expenses, only include the portion you would be paying, not the total amounts. Will your children remain in your home? If so, what provision do you need to pay off the mortgage, if you still have one? How much debt do you have that would need to be paid off?

Children's College _____ x _____ = _____
Education   Per year   Number of years   Total amount

Mortgage Pay-off   = _____
                                                       Total amount

Debts   = _____
                                                       Total amount

Other   = _____
                                                       Total amount

Total income needed (add all totals in section 2)   _____
                                                       Total amount

3. *Other Expenses To Pay for Your Minor Children*

Look over your budget and determine which areas will need to be continued for your children. For example, if your children live with the other parent, how much will you need to provide for their on-going care? What if they live with another relative or friend? How much medical coverage will you need to provide? What sports or activities will they continue?

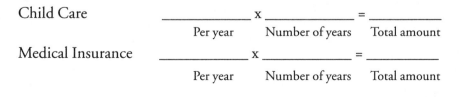

Child Care   _____ x _____ = _____
                   Per year   Number of years   Total amount

Medical Insurance _____ x _____ = _____
                   Per year   Number of years   Total amount

Activities _____ x _____ = _____
               Per year   Number of years   Total amount

Other   _____ x _____ = _____
               Per year   Number of years   Total amount

Other   _____ x _____ = _____
               Per year   Number of years   Total amount

Total Expenses (add all totals in section 3)   _____
                                                   Total amount

Add section 2 total   _____
And section 3 total   + _____
Total expenses   = _____
Deduct section 1 total   − _____
Income still needed   = _____

4. *Assets That Could Be Used To Provide for Your Children*

Home equity can only be counted as an asset if the house is to be sold after your death. If your home is to be sold, how much equity will your children receive? Do you have personal possessions that can be sold? Enter only the amounts your children would receive.

Home Equity   = _____
                                          Total amount

Real Estate   = _____
                                          Total amount

Investments   = _____
                                          Total amount

Annuities   = _____
                                          Total amount

Savings   = _____
                                          Total amount

Retirement Benefits   = _____
                                          Total amount

Personal Possessions   = _____

Total amount

Trusts   _____ x _____ = _____

Per year   Number of years   Total amount

Total Assets (add all totals in section 4)   _____

Total amount

5. *Basic Insurance Required*
Income needed (section 3)   _____

Deduct assets (section 4)   – _____

Insurance needed   = _____

Since this amount reflects your current need, you will need to review this amount on a periodic basis. As the children age and become independent, insurance needs decrease. Plus, other changes in the family can affect insurance needs, such as the death of the other parent, remarriage, inflation, increase in assets, and so on.

Appendix E

BUYING A CAR

O wning a car is a fact of life in our society. To be sure, there are those, particularly in large urban areas, who are able to get around by using public transportation, but the lifestyle of today's average family makes owning at least one car a practical necessity. So, if having a car is a necessity, what is the most economical way of obtaining it?

PRELIMINARY STEPS

1. Examine Your Motives. Let's face it. In the U.S. the majority of new automobile sales are made because of the buyer's wants, not needs. In fact, a significant portion of people who are shopping for a car—new or used—simply don't need it. Often they are just tired of their car, it looks old and out of date, or it needs major repairs to put it back into top condition; or their neighbors, former spouse, or coworkers have gotten new cars. We have been programmed to think that if any of these conditions exists, we are justified in acquiring another, preferably new, car.

Cars do wear out, and everyone will eventually find himself or herself in the position of having to get another car. However, everyone would do well to examine their motives first, because so often the notion to buy a car springs from the emotional, rather than the rational, side of human nature.

2. Determine Your Needs. Having examined your motives, the next step is to determine your needs. Luke 14:28 says, *"For which one of you, when he wants to build a tower, does not first sit down and calculate the cost, to see if he has enough to complete it?"* Most people would naturally like to be sitting behind the wheel of a shiny new automobile. But have they calculated the cost? They need to consider not only the question of whether they can afford it but also whether buying a new car is the best stewardship of their hard-earned money.

Costs (payments, insurance, maintenance) for a mid-range new car commonly run in excess of $400 a month. That kind of expense can wreck the average single parent's budget. Sure, they may be able to make the monthly payments, but the other major budget categories, like Housing, Food, and Clothing, will begin to suffer; and since these are major needs, the single parent inevitably will go into debt to obtain them.

The average single parent needs to have a good-quality, reliable, used car. Of course the size, style, age, and appearance of the car will vary from person to person.

3. Become an Informed Buyer. Doing your homework before you begin can help you find the car best suited to your needs. Consumer advocacy groups and publications, such as *Consumer Reports,* report on the safety, maintenance, and value of the various car models. Remember too that buying cheaper does not always mean a better deal.

Friends and family members are also a good source of information. Talk with owners of cars similar to the model you are considering to see if they are satisfied. Ask your insurance agent if the year and model of car you are considering is a target for thieves.

SHOPPING FOR A USED CAR

From Friends. Once you have determined the type of car you want and can afford, the next step is to find the car. Go to your closest friends first. Let them know you're looking for a car. Find out if there is a Christian family in your church that has a car to sell that will fit your need. Before most Christians will sell their car to somebody they know, they will either reveal everything that is wrong with the car or else have it fixed. By purchasing directly from the owner, you can learn the history of the car and usually negotiate the best possible price.

Leasing or Car Rental Companies. These are a good source of late-model used cars. Many of these companies keep their cars one or two years and then resell them. Most of these cars have been routinely maintained, have low highway mileage, and usually are available for a fair price. Often a car obtained from such a company will come with at least a one-year warranty.

Banks and Credit Unions. Another good source is your local banker. Let your loan processor know that if the bank obtains a really good car as a repossession (the bank has to recover the car) you are interested in buying it. Be aware that a repossessed car probably will need some repairs since its owner most likely couldn't afford to keep it maintained properly. Be sure you have some money in reserve for this purpose. Banks and credit unions sometimes offer special services, such as direct sales to customers or helping you locate a car.

Car Dealers. Dealers have the largest selection of used cars available. A used car that was locally owned can be a good deal, especially if you are able to contact the previous owner to see if there are any hidden problems with the car.

Although most car dealers are honest, some dishonest ones give the industry a bad name. Buyers need to beware and prepare themselves so that they will know when dealers are trying to take advantage of them. I recommend the book, *What Car Dealers Don't Want You to Know,* by Mark Eskeldson (Technews Publishing, 1995), as a useful tool when considering buying a car from a dealer.

Advertisements. A fifth source is advertisements through daily newspapers, car trader publications, and shopper's publications. The difficulty in going through this source is that you don't know the seller, and the seller doesn't know you. Unfortunately, there are a lot of unethical, dishonest people out there that have cars for sale.

Before buying any used car, it is advisable to write an affidavit saying, "I swear that, to my knowledge, the car I am selling has no obvious defects or rust and the mileage on the odometer is accurate." Have the seller sign it (before a notary if possible). Most honest people won't object, and most dishonest ones won't sign it.

Finally, have a mechanic check the car you are purchasing for defects or problems that may not be obvious to you, such as hidden rust, signs of having been in an accident, and engine problems. The dollars you spend up front having a mechanic look at the car can save you much grief and expense later.

ABOUT FINANCING YOUR CAR

The best way to finance a car is *not* to finance it. It is always the best policy to save the money and pay cash for your car. Auto financing is poor stewardship at the very best. But, assuming that there are those who, for some reason or another, feel they must finance the purchase of their car, there are some basic guidelines that should be followed.

1.   Do not finance through a car dealership, if at all possible.

Arranging a loan through a bank or other financial institution can allow you to negotiate with the dealer on a cash basis. When you do arrange a loan, be sure it is a simple interest loan with no payoff restrictions. Then at least you have the option to become debt free in a shorter period of time.

2.   Do not trade in your old car; sell it instead.

If a car dealer can sell your car and make a profit, so can you. It certainly takes more time and effort to sell your car, but it is worth it. Advertise your car in the newspaper classifieds (or a local shopper paper) or put a sign in the car window. Provided your car is in reasonable shape, it shouldn't take very long to sell.

3.   If your old car is not paid off, keep it until it is.

If you trade in a car with a mortgage on it, you are simply taking your current debt and refinancing it into a new car, effectively doubling the amount of interest you have been paying on your old loan.

ANSWERS TO QUESTIONS
ABOUT BUYING A CAR

Should I buy an extended warranty on my new car?

If you are considering an extended warranty, there are several questions you need to ask. First, does the warranty cover a period of time or a number of miles that is not covered under any implied warranties? Second, does the extended warranty cover parts and labor or parts only? Third, does the price of the extended warranty seem reasonable in relation to the price of the parts covered?

If an extended warranty covers five years or 50,000 miles, then the average driver really will get coverage only for approximately three years since the average person drives more than 10,000 miles per year. A better warranty would cover five years or 100,000 miles.

If only parts are covered, the cost of labor is usually so great that the owner will not get the full benefit of buying the extended warranty, unless each part covered is more expensive than the relative cost of the warranty.

How much of our family's budget should be designated for car expenses?

About 15 to 17 percent of your *Net Spendable Income (NSI)* should be allotted for automobile expenses. That includes payments, gasoline, oil, maintenance, and insurance.

If you simply do not have the funds in your budget to repair or replace your car, I encourage you to talk to your church about your need. Many churches now offer car care ministries to help single parents maintain their automobiles. If your car needs to be replaced, the church still may be able to help you. A church occasionally will receive a car as a donation that is designated for someone in need. Sometimes the church will let their members know when one member has a specific need. Also, a few ministries for single parents accept donations of used cars for single parents.

What about leasing a car?

Leasing a car often seems attractive to those who cannot otherwise afford a new car, because it involves little or no money down, low interest rates, and low monthly payments for the length of the lease agreement. Because of these incentives, buyers pay very little toward the actual value of the car.

Cars usually are leased for two to three years, and the lessee is urged to turn the car back in to the dealer and lease another new car at the end of the lease, rather than finance the remaining debt on the car.

If you decide to keep a car when the lease is over, you'll discover you owe a lot more than the car is worth and may have difficulty finding financing, other than through the dealer.

Remember, you never own a car you are leasing; it belongs to the leasing company, and they hold the title. A lease contract is just as binding as a purchase contract and places the lessee in a position of surety. If you continue leasing cars, you will just continue to pay on cars that never are really yours.

That means, if you run into unexpected financial problems during the lease, you can't sell the car. Even if the leasing company would arrange for the sale of the car (and it is under no obligation to do so), almost always the amount owed on the lease is more than the car is worth, leaving the lessee with no car and still owing more money!

What is surety?

There are over twenty references in Proverbs to the principle of surety. *Surety* is taking on an obligation to pay for something without an absolutely certain way to pay for it. To avoid surety, the best policy is to never borrow; but if you do borrow, be sure that the item for which you borrowed is total collateral and that you would not be liable for any deficiency beyond that.

SUMMARY

Honestly evaluate your real need for a car. If you determine your need justifies a purchase, buy a used car. Generally speaking, it is a much better buy. Shop for value instead of the lowest price. Save for your car and pay cash. However, if you must borrow, go through an institution other than the dealership. Arrange for a simple interest loan with no payoff restrictions. Then negotiate with the dealer on a cash basis. Finally, rather than trading your old car in, sell it yourself.

Appendix F

HOUSING

Since the cost of buying or renting suitable housing for your family is perhaps the greatest expense you'll ever incur, you must study your personal situation, research the possibilities, and pray for the Lord's guidance in order to make an educated decision about finding what's right for you.

CONSIDER THE VARIABLES

Before you decide whether to rent or buy a house, determine how much you can afford to spend. If you are not actively living on a budget, you should make this your first step. *The Financial Guide for the Single Parent* workbook is excellent for helping you set up a written financial plan.

Although your financial situation will be the major factor in determining what type of housing you need, there are other variables that must be considered. Prayerfully give the following questions some thought.

1. *Is your job secure enough to take on a mortgage?*
   If not, consider renting instead of buying a house.

2. *How long do you plan to stay in the area?*
   If you know you will be staying in the community for an extend-

ed time—five to seven years at least—home ownership may be a good option.

3. *What is the economy like in the area you are considering? Is the area growing substantially and will the house appreciate?*
You don't want to be stuck with a house that you can't sell because of a poor economy.

4. *What is the cost of living in the new area?*
If it is high, it will definitely affect your budget and may change the amount you can afford for housing.

After answering these questions, take the amount you can spend for housing and determine if house payments, including taxes and insurance, would be equal to or less than rental payments for a similar house in the same area. If they would be, then buying a home may be a wise choice.

BIBLICAL PRINCIPLES TO CONSIDER

Borrowing. God doesn't prohibit borrowing, but He certainly does discourage it. In fact, every biblical reference to it is a negative one. Consider Proverbs 22:7, *"The rich rules over the poor, and the borrower becomes the lender's slave."* Homeowners who lose their jobs and are unable to keep up with the payments find out firsthand what it's like to be in the position of a slave. Remember, borrowing is literally a vow to repay, and God requires that we keep our vows.

Surety. Another biblical principle that affects you when you borrow money is "surety." Proverbs 17:18 says, *"A man lacking in sense pledges, and becomes surety in the presence of his neighbor."* Surety is simply taking on an obligation to pay later without a certain way to pay it. For example, if you buy a house and pay a 5 percent down payment and finance 95 percent, then the real estate market only needs to decrease 5 percent for you to risk being caught in surety. But if you put 20 to 30 percent down on a house and finance 80 to 70 percent, your risk of being caught in surety is not as great. If you're going to borrow to buy, accumulate enough for a sizable down payment.

The best way to avoid surety, however, is to be sure that any money you borrow is fully collateralized. Suppose you bought land that cost $10,000, and you put $1,000 down and borrowed $9,000. The terms of your contract should stipulate, "If I can't pay for this land, I give you the right to take the land back and keep all the money I've paid in, but I'm released from all personal liabilities."

A statement that releases you from personal liability for the loan is called an *exculpatory clause*. Unfortunately, most institutions hold you personally responsible for mortgages and don't allow exculpatory clauses in their contracts. Surety is a biblical principle, not a law, but it will certainly come to haunt you when you can least afford it.

RENTING A HOUSE

If you have decided that renting a house is a better option for you at this time, there are several things to consider. First, decide what type of dwelling you want to rent. You can rent a house, apartment, townhouse, mobile home, or even a room or suite in someone's house. The people in your church are often a good source of information about availability, location, and cost of rentals around the area.

Types of Leases

There are two main types of leases. One is a month-to-month lease, and the other is a lease for a specified amount of time—usually six months or one year. The month-to-month lease is great if you aren't sure how long you will be in the area or if you are waiting for a house to be finished. The problem with this type of lease is that the rent can be raised with simply a 30-day notice. You can avoid this problem with a six-month or yearly lease. The rental price is renegotiated at the end of the lease term, and you can choose to stay and pay more or move out.

Deposits

A security deposit is usually required when you sign a lease. This deposit can be retained by the owner if you damage the property while you are renting or if you have to move before your lease is up. A cleaning, pet, or key deposit also may be required. These are usually refunded when you turn in your keys and the owner inspects the property.

Renter's Insurance

The purpose of renter's insurance is threefold. It covers the value of your furniture and personal belongings, protects you from being sued by the owner's insurance company if there is damage to the property (grease fire or water damage), and it covers the liability if someone else is hurt on the property because of your or your children's negligence (someone falls or trips over a toy and is injured). Content and liability insurance usually costs about $100 to $150 a year and is well worth it, unless you can afford to replace all your belongings and have plenty of money on hand to cover exposed liabilities.

BUYING A HOUSE

If you've determined that purchasing a house fits into your budget and is in your best interest long term, you can begin to look at the options available to you. You might consider these different types of dwellings: houses, including a new house or rebuilding a "fixer-upper"; condominiums; mobile homes; or prebuilt homes.

House. First you will need to decide whether you want to purchase a new or used house. The advantages of building a new house are that you can design your house to fit your individual needs and locate it where you want it. The disadvantages of a new house are, with few exceptions, those who build a new house end up spending more money than they planned. Changes made while the house is being built cost a lot of money, and it takes considerable time and mental effort to oversee the construction of a new house. Habitat for Humanity has provided new homes with interest-free loans to many single parents who were willing to put in "sweat equity."

The advantages of buying a used house are that you know exactly what it is going to cost, and you can get more extras. Used houses usually come with curtains, curtain rods, towel racks, lights in the closets, light bulbs, an established lawn, shrubbery, and, occasionally, appliances. Be sure the contract states exactly which items will come with the house.

The disadvantages of a used house are that, usually, when a house has been lived in, it will have some wear and tear. The older the house, the more things that will need repair. You always should check the heating and air conditioning, roof, hot water heater, and appliances to see if they are in working condition. You may choose to hire someone to do this for you. Then you can decide whether to purchase the house as is or back out of the deal.

The fixer-upper or handyman's special. Another alternative is a fixer-upper. This type of a house can be purchased at a relatively lower cost than other previously owned houses. But you will need to take into consideration the additional funds required outside of the normal housing allocation for repairs. Be sure to check the house thoroughly, including foundation, plumbing, and wiring, so you know exactly what is wrong with the house before you buy it. If you have the skills and don't mind doing the repairs, you can make a nice profit when you sell it.

Condominiums. Another option is a condominium. You need to be aware of some additional costs involved above the purchase price, such as maintenance fees, club fees, and any other amenities available in the private community. Be aware that the maintenance fees are subject to change each year, and you have no control over them. This is not a bad option, especially if you don't want to bother with yard work.

Mobile homes or prebuilt homes. Although some people won't consider living in manufactured homes because of preconceived notions about this type of housing, many couples (and single parents) have purchased mobile homes and think they are great. It gives them better housing than they could afford otherwise and satisfies the needs of their families.

The major disadvantage of manufactured housing is the depreciation. A new manufactured home will lose about 25 percent of its total value when it leaves the sales lot. Consider purchasing a previously owned manufactured home, because someone else has already taken the depreciation.

PURCHASE OPTIONS

Now that you've decided what type of house you want to buy, you need to decide how to pay for it. In order to serve God in the very best way, the goal of all Christians should be to become debt free—including their homes. If you choose to borrow money to purchase a home, you should make it your goal to pay it off as soon as possible. There are several ways to do this that will be discussed later.

Pay cash. The best way to buy is to pay cash if you are financially able. The idea of owning a home debt free is not a new one; in fact, it's quite ancient. Most families used to own their houses, and those who didn't were abnormal. Those who couldn't afford the large house they wanted simply bought a smaller one, put a great deal of time and effort into it, improved its value, sold it, and then upscaled.

Institutional loans. Loans are available through banks, savings and loans, credit unions, or mortgage companies. If you have to borrow to buy your house, an institutional loan is perhaps the most common type of loan, although it may not necessarily be the best type for you. It's very important to shop around with this type of loan, because there are so many variables. As you enter the marketplace of home buyers, you should know what type of loans are available to you and what additional costs are associated with each.

Fees and contracts. Most institutional loans require a down payment—usually anywhere between 5 and 20 percent, but you can and should put more down if possible. There are also various closing costs. Closing costs can include loan origination fees, points, attorneys' fees, survey fees, appraisal fees, PMI (private mortgage insurance), real estate commissions, credit reports, title search fees, and more. These fees can add up to quite an expense—several thousand dollars—and should be researched thoroughly when considering any loan. Many times the seller may pay for some or all of the closing costs.

If your offer to purchase the home is subject to selling your present home, getting financial approval, or waiting on results from various inspections, including radon gas testing, termite inspections, appliance and structural inspections, or water testing, be sure these contingencies are spelled out in the contract.

Fixed rate mortgages are an excellent form of home loan. You know exactly what the interest rate and monthly mortgage payment will be and if it will fit into your budget. Although a fixed rate loan will have slightly higher interest rates than other types of loans, it will not change during the life of the loan. You will know that the terms are for the next 15 or 30 years. Shop around for the lowest interest rate, since they do vary from institution to institution and from week to week.

Adjustable rate mortgages (ARM) are not a bad form of home loan, provided you can get an interest rate lower than the prevailing fixed rate and the loan contains a cap on the maximum increase during the life of the loan. These loans fluctuate with the economy; therefore it's very important to know exactly how high the interest rate could go. Most ARMs begin with an interest rate that's a percentage point or two below current fixed rate loans; then they are adjusted every year after that. This makes it possible for more couples to qualify for these types of loans, but makes it hard to establish exactly how much to budget for housing expenses from year to year.

Be sure you understand the terms before you choose this type of loan. For example, if you can get an 11 percent ARM with a 5 percent cap—or a maximum rate of 16 percent—and the current fixed rate is 13 percent, you would be better off accepting the ARM than the fixed rate mortgage. However, you need to figure out what your monthly payment would be if the interest rate rose to 16 percent. Would that payment fit into your budget comfortably?

One last point to consider on adjustable rate loans is the duration of the loan. Many of these loans are short-term loans that carry a balloon payment (typically due in seven years). Therefore, I don't advise them for most people, unless you know you can pay off the home in that amount of time. There is no guarantee you'll be able to renegotiate another loan you can afford, and you could lose your home.

Payday mortgages are designed to increase the frequency of your loan payments. Instead of paying a monthly payment, the home buyer pays one-half the monthly payment every other week or one-quarter of the payment every week. Since more of the payment is applied to the principal, equity is accrued at a faster rate. This will consequently reduce the life of the loan and the borrower reaps the benefits of paying less interest and paying off the mortgage early. Some lenders don't offer this type of loan because they lose interest. However, this financing option is becoming more popular due to increasing competition.

Compare a $60,000 mortgage at 12 percent.

	P/I	Life of Loan (Yrs.)	Interest Paid	Interest Saved
Weekly	$154.29	18.79	$ 90,809.33	$71,362.20
Bi-weekly	$308.59	19.04	$ 92,752.05	$69,429.15
Conventional	$627.27	30	$162,181.20	–0–

An *assumable mortgage* is an existing mortgage that is assumed by the buyer at the existing terms of the seller's loan. Assumable mortgages benefit the buyer because the interest rate and mortgage payment are usually lower than current rates. Check to see if there is an assumption fee and if the loan will be assumable if you sell the home to someone else.

FINANCING

Government financing. Purchasing a house with a loan subsidized by the government may be a matter of concern to some people. Although there are no biblical principles that specifically apply to this subject, it is my personal opinion that Christians should not look to the government for help but rather to God. By depending on the government to supply more and more of our basic needs, I fear this eventually will take away from our trust in God. If you have prayed about it and still feel you should take advantage of the subsidized loan, then by all means follow the conscience the Lord gave you.

There are several types of government loans that may be obtained through your local banking institution. VA, FHA, and state-bonded programs are attractive to home buyers because of the low interest rates and the low down payment required. Be careful not to get yourself into surety with these types of loans.

Seller financing. Available in land sales contract, trust deed, and so on. Another way to purchase is for the seller to finance the home for the buyer. This provides a steady income to the seller, and the buyer usually gets the financing for a percent or two lower than current interest rates and saves on closing costs. Be sure a qualified attorney draws up all legal papers so there is no question about the terms of the sale.

Equity sharing. This is an excellent way for someone to get help in purchasing a home and for an investor to receive a healthy return on a relatively small investment. This is the way it works. Someone needing help in obtaining funds for a down payment on a mortgage locates an investor willing to provide a certain portion of those funds. A written agreement is drawn up that defines the amount of years the house will be retained by the buyer and the amount of equity that will be paid to the investor once the house is sold. Usually the investor will receive his full investment back plus 50 percent of any profit.

A provision should be made so that if the buyer wants to keep the home after a period of years, the investor will be repaid with a predetermined amount of interest on his original loan. In order to avoid any differences, a good Christian attorney should be involved in the preparation of any equity-sharing plan.

Parent-assisted financing. It is our responsibility as parents to help our children—reasonably. For example, a parent pays the down payment for a son or daughter to buy a home. The home is in joint ownership; the parent owns part of it, and the child owns part. The parent then rents the home back to the child. The parent receives the income, depreciates the house, and takes it off his or her taxes; the child rents it, retains partial ownership, and profits from the eventual sale. The child should provide the repairs and maintenance needed. This method benefits both parent and child and may also be used by Christians willing to help single parents (non-family members) get their own house.

Parents with substantial savings may choose to be the lender for their single-parent children. This method will save money on closing costs and can be a source of retirement income for the parents. Be sure, however, that the single-parent children are mature enough to be responsible for this generosity and that they do not take advantage of you. All legal forms should be drawn up and on record so there are no questions if the parents or the children pass away or in the event of default. Parental financing should be viewed by both parties with the same financial commitment and the same consequences as any other type of financing.

SELLING YOUR HOUSE

If you are on the other side of the coin and are selling a home instead of purchasing one, there are certain things you should know. First, you must decide who is going to sell it.

By owner. You can elect to sell your home yourself in order to save the cost of a real estate agent's commission. This means you will advertise it yourself and must be available to show the house to interested buyers. Be knowledgeable about selling. Know what other homes in your area are selling for and understand what you must do when someone contracts to buy it. Have a qualified attorney review all offers before you sign anything.

By real estate agent. You may choose to have an agent sell your home for you. This will give you greater exposure in the real estate market. It may save you time and money because the agent can advertise, use the Multiple Listing Service, and show the place while you are at work. You will have to pay the agent's commission—around 5 to 10 percent of the selling price—if your home sells. Have the broker explain every offer that is made for the purchase of your home. You may choose to have an attorney review all offers if you are not knowledgeable about real estate.

Other Considerations When Selling Your Home

Tax consequences. If you sell your home and buy another that costs less than the one you sold, you must pay a capital gains tax on the difference between the two. However, there are allowances for selling costs and improvements that can reduce the gain. You may postpone tax payment if you buy a more expensive home within two years. There also is a one-time exclusion on capital gains for those over 55 years old. You may want to contact a professional accountant or tax advisor for additional help.

Continued liability. You can be held liable for any loan a buyer assumes from you if the buyer defaults, unless you obtain a total release from liability. Contact the lending institution for more information about obtaining one of these releases. Check to see if there is a fee involved.

Earnest money contracts:. When someone is genuinely interested in buying your home, that person will submit a contract and earnest money. This is a deposit so you won't sell it to anyone else while the potential buyer is getting financing approved, selling his or her home, or awaiting inspection results. At this time you should be willing to explain any problems or situations the buyer should know about. Not only will it save the buyer some headaches down the road, but you will be setting a wonderful Christian example. This is also the time to declare which items will be included in the purchase price. Some items to consider are appliances, curtains, swing sets, firewood, or maintenance equipment. You may desire to present a counter offer, showing any terms of their offer you are unwilling to accept.

QUESTIONS ABOUT REFINANCING

Should I refinance to obtain a lower interest rate?

If you are considering refinancing your house to take advantage of lower interest rates, determine if it will actually save you money by figuring the dollar amount of interest you will save, compared to the costs involved in refinancing. Some banks will require new title searches, surveys, and appraisals to refinance your loan. If you can easily reclaim these expenses through the savings in interest within a few years, refinancing is for you. You usually will benefit through refinancing if the new interest rate is at least 3 percent lower than your present mortgage.

THE FINANCIAL GUIDE FOR THE SINGLE PARENT

Should I get a home equity loan (second mortgage) to pay off my consumer debts?

Proverbs 3:27-28 says, *"Do not withhold good from those to whom it is due, when it is in your power to do it. Do not say to your neighbor, 'Go, and come back, and tomorrow I will give it,' when you have it with you."* If you can't pay your bills on a regular basis and you have the means to pay those bills, God requires that you do whatever it takes to pay them off.

Unfortunately, borrowing more money, especially against the equity in your home, doesn't usually solve the problem. It only treats a symptom of the problem. You must treat the problem itself. If you are having problems with your credit cards, cut them up. Establish a budgeted payment plan and repay each creditor. Work at paying off the smaller debt first, then the next, and so on. Remember, the borrower becomes the lender's slave.

OTHER QUESTIONS ABOUT REAL ESTATE

What happens if the bank forecloses on my house?

Although foreclosure is a serious problem, it does not mean God has washed His hands of you. As a result of losing a home, you will learn a costly, yet valuable, lesson on the danger of surety. And although you may not be held legally responsible for the difference between the amount of your mortgage and the price the lender receives from the sale of your home, you are morally responsible for this debt. When you enter into a contract, you are bound by your word to fulfill its intent. Remember Psalm 37:21. Once the foreclosure has been finalized, work out a payment plan for the balance that will fit into your adjusted budget.

The lender has the option to file a deficiency judgment against you and may retain this right for several years. Check your state laws. He or she also may choose to release you from the deficiency debt. The lender is the master and has this right. You must commit to pay the deficiency and to do whatever the lender requests.

If you are fortunate enough to deed the home to the lender instead of being foreclosed on, you may avoid paying anything, but you will still lose the home and the equity. If you have fallen behind on your payment or must move quickly, make every effort to sell your home, even if you have to take a loss. Since foreclosed dwellings are generally sold at auction for much less than fair market value, you often can sell it for more, thus reducing the amount you must pay back.

What type of insurance should I have on my home?

Most lending institutions require that you have enough insurance to cover the amount of the mortgage. A homeowner's insurance policy is a comprehensive insurance plan covering the home, its contents, and any liability associated with the property. Usually the homeowner's policy is the least expensive way to insure a dwelling. You can get a fire policy only, but it isn't as comprehensive as a homeowner's policy. Shop around before you buy any kind of insurance, because there can be a significant amount of difference in the cost of insurance from one company to another.

If you are going to buy a condominium or mobile home, most insurance companies provide specialized insurance for these types of dwellings.

Should I have life insurance to cover my home?

It is very wise for a family to have life insurance to pay off their house. This insurance is commonly called *mortgage life insurance.*

Mortgage life insurance is usually sold through the lender from whom you received your home loan. This can be a very expensive way to purchase life insurance. A decreasing term insurance policy through your local insurance agent may be less expensive.

The best option would be to determine what your total life insurance needs are and include your home loan balance with this. By purchasing one policy, versus several, you will save money. As your need for death protection diminishes, you can reduce your coverage.

What types of prepayment options are available?

After you have made your regular monthly payment, any additional funds you put toward your mortgage go directly to the principal, exclusive of any interest. Therefore, the next month you're paying slightly less interest and slightly more principal on the unpaid balance. Each month that you prepay part of the principal, a greater amount goes toward the principal the following month, since your regular payment amount stays constant. By this prepayment method, if you pay an additional $100 per month, a $60,000 mortgage at 10 percent for 30 years can be reduced by approximately $68,500 and 16 years.

You may want to write two separate checks, one for the regular monthly payment and one for the additional principal. Write "principal" on this check to be sure there is no confusion at the lending institution.

$60,000 mortgage at 10 percent.

	P/I	Life of Loan (Yrs.)	Interest Paid	Interest Saved
Conventional	$526	30	$129,360	–0–
Additional $100	$626	16	$ 60,818	$68,542
Additional $50	$576	20	$ 78,240	$51,120
Additional $25	$551	23.8	$ 97,586	$31,774

Another prepay option available is a *payday* mortgage. Refer to the paragraph under "Institutional Loans" on page 222.

Before making any prepayments on your mortgage, check with your lending institution about any penalties and request an annual amortization schedule to monitor the reduction in your principal balance.

Many families will be able to make extra monthly principal payments—$50, $100—and pay their loans off earlier than scheduled. This may be the simplest option for most families.

Is buying foreclosed homes ethical?

Are we guilty of robbing the poor (condemned in God's Word) when we take over foreclosed homes? You must first ask yourself, "Did I help to cause the problems that generated the foreclosure?" In other words, did you lend somebody money they could not pay back and then foreclose on the home? If so, you would be guilty of robbing the poor.

The second question that you have to ask is, "Am I being fair?"

Have I willfully taken advantage of someone else's misery? In practical fact, these people are going to lose their homes regardless of whether you buy them out of foreclosure, because the bank is going to foreclose. As long as you did not generate the foreclosure, there is nothing scripturally wrong with buying a foreclosed dwelling. If you can get to the family before they get into foreclosure, you could save them some money they might lose otherwise. Remember what Paul wrote. *"Do nothing from selfishness or empty conceit, but with humility of mind let each of you regard one another as more important than himself"* (Philippians 2:3).

Is a debt-free home realistic for a single parent?

One of the essential foundation blocks of a biblically oriented financial plan is a debt-free home. This should be the goal of all Christians. Anything can happen to this economy. It may be a collapse or hyperinflation brought on by printing massive amounts of money to avoid a depression. Either way, you can lose whatever is indebted. A debt-free home is yours, not the lender's.

Personally, I would do whatever is necessary to become debt free. It may mean selling a larger house and paring down expenses by buying a smaller, debt-free home. I would recommend that. We are a nation of debtors, and eventually we will grasp the meaning of Proverbs 22:7, *"The rich rules over the poor, and the borrower becomes the lender's slave."*

To a great extent, your circumstances will determine whether you should buy a home. Don't put yourself in jeopardy just to own a home. If you have a certain way to pay for it, then it may be a good idea.

Should I pay off my mortgage and lose the tax deduction?

People who borrow to purchase homes often believe that the tax breaks they receive justify the interest that is paid. Those who are in the 28 percent tax bracket and pay $1,000 in interest in a year may receive a $280 tax credit. This obviously shows that $720 went into someone else's pocket—the lender's. The best alternative is to pay off your home mortgage as early as possible and not only save the interest but accumulate a sizable savings. This far outweighs any tax deductions you may receive from paying interest.

Appendix G

CHECKLIST OF
IMPORTANT DOCUMENTS

CHECKLIST OF IMPORTANT DOCUMENTS

WILLS

Will For	Dated	Attorney	Location of Will

POWER OF ATTORNEY

Power of Attorney For	Power Given To	Date	Location of Document

BIRTH CERTIFICATES

Certificate For	Date of Birth	Certificate Number	Location of Certificate

DEATH CERTIFICATES

Certificate For	Date of Death	Certificate Number	Location of Certificate

MARRIAGE LICENSES

License For	Date of Marriage	Certificate Number	Location of Document

DIVORCE DECREES

Divorce Decree For	Date of Divorce	Decree Number	Location of Document

SOCIAL SECURITY RECORDS

Social Security Records/Card For	Social Security No.	Date Received	Location of Document

REAL ESTATE RECORDS

Records For Property Located At	Type of Record	Dated	Location of Document

AUTOMOBILE RECORDS

Title & Registration For Vehicle	Title Number	Dated	Location of Document

LIFE INSURANCE POLICIES

Policy on Life Of	Policy Number	Company	Location of Document

BANK, SAVINGS & LOAN, OR CREDIT UNION RECORDS

Name of Institution	Type of Account	Account Numbere	Location of Document

SAFETY DEPOSIT BOXES

Box Registered In Name Of	Name of Institution	Box Number	Location of Keys

CHURCH RECORDS

Type of Record	Record For (Name)	Date of Event	Location of Document

MILITARY RECORDS

Type of Record	Record For (Name)	Date of Event	Location of Document

OTHER IMPORTANT PAPERS

Type of Record	For	Dated	Location of Document

Christian Financial Concepts Inc.

Teaching | Biblical Principles of Managing Money

Larry Burkett, founder and president of Christian Financial Concepts, is the best-selling author of 49 books on business and personal finances and two novels. He also hosts two radio programs broadcast on hundreds of stations worldwide.

Larry earned B.S. degrees in marketing and in finance, and recently an Honorary Doctorate in Economics was conferred by Southwest Baptist University. For several years Larry served as a manager in the space program at Cape Canaveral, Florida. He also has been vice president of an electronics manufacturing firm. Larry's education, business experience, and solid understanding of God's Word enable him to give practical, Bible-based financial counsel to families, churches, and businesses.

Founded in 1976, Christian Financial Concepts, Inc. is a nonprofit, nondenominational ministry dedicated to helping God's people gain a clear understanding of how to manage their money according to scriptural principles. Although practical assistance is provided on many levels, the purpose of CFC is simply *to bring glory to God by freeing His people from financial bondage so they may serve Him to their utmost.*

One major avenue of ministry involves the training of volunteers in budget and debt counseling and linking them with financially troubled families and individuals through a nationwide referral network. CFC also provides financial management seminars and workshops for churches and other groups. (Formats available include audio, video, and live instruction.) A full line of printed and audiovisual materials related to money management is available through CFC's materials department (1-800-722-1976) or via the Internet (http://www.cfcministry.org).

Career Pathways, another outreach of Christian Financial Concepts, helps teenagers and adults find their occupational calling. The Career Pathways "assessment" gauges a person's work priorities, skills, vocational interests, and personality. Reports in each of these areas define a person's strengths, weaknesses, and unique, God-given pattern for work.

Visit CFC's Internet site at http://www.cfcministry.org or write to the address below for further information.

Christian Financial Concepts
PO Box 2458
Gainesville, GA 30503-2458

Editing:
Adeline Griffith
Christian Financial Concepts
Gainesville, Georgia

Text Design:
Ragont Design
Rolling Meadows, Illinois

Cover Design:
Ragont Design
Rolling Meadows, Illinois

Printing and Binding:
Quebecor Printing Martinsburg
Martinsburg, West Virginia